A Notebook for Viola Players

A Notebook for Viola Players

Ivo-Jan van der Werff

OXFORD
UNIVERSITY PRESS

OXFORD

UNIVERSITY PRESS

Oxford University Press is a department of the University of Oxford. It furthers
the University's objective of excellence in research, scholarship, and education
by publishing worldwide. Oxford is a registered trade mark of Oxford University
Press in the UK and certain other countries.

Published in the United States of America by Oxford University Press
198 Madison Avenue, New York, NY 10016, United States of America.

© Oxford University Press 2022

CIP data is on file at the Library of Congress
ISBN 978–0–19–761944–5 (pbk.)
ISBN 978–0–19–761943–8 (hbk.)

DOI: 10.1093/oso/9780197619438.001.0001

9 8 7 6 5 4 3 2 1

Paperback printed by Sheridan Books, Inc., United States of America
Hardback printed by Bridgeport National Bindery, Inc., United States of America

Contents

Acknowledgments • vii
About the Companion Website • ix

1   Introduction • 1

2   How to Practice • 7

3   Performance Tips • 14

4   Posture • 23

5   Right Hand • 27

6   Left hand • 50

7   Conclusion • 124

Index • 133

Acknowledgments

I first came across many of the exercises, ideas, and general philosophy in this book while studying with the great viola player and pedagogue Bruno Giuranna. I would like to offer him my thanks for allowing me to reproduce in my own way so much of what he taught us. Right-hand exercises 1 and 3 plus left-hand exercises 1–4 and 6–8 are what he demonstrated to us in his studio. The rest are my own but very much based on the principles he taught.

I would also like to express thanks in particular to my very first viola teacher, Brian Masters, for kindly reading the Notebook through and making many helpful suggestions.

I must also thank my students at the Royal College of Music, London, and the Shepherd School of Music, Rice University, Houston, for being so patient as I bombarded them with yet more sheets of paper as I made numerous revisions.

My final thanks must go to my former Shepherd School students Lynsey Anderson, Carey Skinner, and Bailey Kufchak, and last, to Dr. Michael Tsang, DPT, MM-Musician Injury Management/Prevention Programs: Lynsey, for helping so much in giving sensible suggestions on layout and wording in order to make the book work more effectively; Carey, for taking notes during technique classes on my summer viola retreats, which added many ideas on how to practice and work on the exercises more effectively; Bailey, for adding some great ideas and thoughts in the Wellness and Performance Anxiety sections; and Dr. Tsang, for adding to and reinforcing many of my ideas with his expert knowledge on musicians' physical and mental issues and overall well-being. Video production was by Francis Schmidt.

About the Companion Website

www.oup.com/us/anotebookforviolaplayers

Oxford has created a Web site to accompany *A Notebook for Viola Players*. Material that cannot be made available in a book is provided here, namely video demonstrations of the lessons and exercises in the book. We encourage you to consult this resource in conjunction with the chapters. Examples available online are indicated in the text with Oxford's symbol ⊙

Chapter 1

Introduction

The number of ways to play the viola are determined by the number of violists in the world. Each player has (and should have) a unique technique, a unique sound, and a unique way of interpreting music. Why should this be? Because every violist is physically, emotionally, and mentally individual. It would be so boring if every violist sounded the same—a unique voice is much more interesting and compelling. To this end we have to determine our approach to playing on every level. The basics of what we do are going to be very similar, but the individuality comes later, when we can develop our techniques to express ourselves as unique voices. The basics are determined by the fact that the majority of us are born with two arms, two hands, two thumbs, eight fingers, two legs, etc. In an analogous way, we all walk in a similar fashion, though everyone has an "individual" and often recognizable walk. The physical movement involved in walking is based on common principles for almost everyone. So it should be in the way we set up the viola and how we approach it.

The position of the body, the way we stand or sit, the way we raise our arms to hold the viola and bow, the actual bow hold, the shape of the left hand: all these basic things can be approached from common physical principles, even though every player is built differently. The wonderful thing about violists is not just the physical diversity of the people playing the viola but also the diversity in the shape and size of violas themselves. This lack of standardization of the viola can lead to challenging issues and individual resolutions to problems. Again, coming from common principles can help in deciding on all the variations of approaches we have.

I am tall, 6′ 3″, and have long arms and large hands. Many of my students are envious of my size because large stretches of the left hand are not such an issue for me. However, because my fingers are large, I find it difficult to play chords where there is one stopped note between one or two open strings. An example is in the 3rd movement of the Shostakovich Sonata, bar 11, where I literally cannot play

A Notebook for Viola Players. Ivo-Jan van der Werff, Oxford University Press. © Oxford University Press 2022.
DOI: 10.1093/oso/9780197619438.003.0001

the first pizzicato chord of D B (open)D. My 2nd finger touches either the C string or the open D string. My solution is to finger it 1,3,0 instead of the usual 1,2,0. I can place the 3rd finger more upright than the 2nd and hence it can clear the strings on either side. This is a perfect example of what I mean when I say that we sometimes have to find individual solutions to problems.

To this end, it is very important that we don't overstretch or overexert ourselves in the physical pursuit of technical freedom and fluency. If you have shorter arms and literally cannot get to the tip of the bow, don't worry about it. It is practically impossible to create a really smooth bow change when the right arm is stretched as far as it can go. Change bow where it is comfortable and get used to using slightly less bow. It may be that holding the bow an inch or so higher might help in utilizing a true whole bow, or holding the viola slightly more in front of you can also help. You have to find what works best on your particular viola and bow. It's also possible that those with smaller hands may have issues holding all the fingers of the left hand down as suggested in some of the exercises. Again, this need not be a big issue. Obviously, holding the fingers down has its benefits, but the most important thing is to be able to move your hand fluently and with good intonation. You might consider where you balance your left hand: stretching back from the 2nd finger can give more range of movement provided the hand remains flexible. The most important thing is that we all need to find our own optimal way of playing, taking into account our individual characteristics. That is the real purpose of this book.

The one thing that every single violist can hopefully agree on is that we want to create the best sound possible. Why, after all, are we drawn to this amazing instrument, the one closest in pitch and timbre to the human voice? Everything I suggest in the text and the exercises extends to this one, basic, unifying principle. Sound or tone is affected not just by the way we put the bow on the string but also by intonation, the way we hold the viola, the way the fingers of the left hand approach the fingerboard, the quality of vibrato, and the way we stand and breathe. The list goes on and on.

I hope that by reading through the text and playing the exercises in the ways suggested, you will gain a good understanding of how to create a great sound, how to allow the viola to resonate without forcing it, how to gain dexterity in both the bow and the left hand, and how to play in a relaxed yet energized manner, all without undue effort.

Ultimately, everything I suggest about how to play the viola should become natural and habitual. Especially for more advanced players trying this out for the first time, one of the toughest things is to overcome old, ingrained habits. Always remember the goal, don't get discouraged, and don't rush. New habits take time to bed in. The goal is definitely worth the physical and mental effort.

As a final note, much of what I have written is logical and even obvious, but I remember from being a student myself, and having seen countless times as a teacher, that the logical and obvious often disappear from our minds as soon as we start playing the viola, so I will not apologize for this!

A Note to Amateur Viola Players

Although this book comes mainly from my decades of teaching students who aspire to become professional players, I have, over the years, had the pleasure of teaching many enthusiastic amateur players, and I hope that this book can also be of use to them. Though some exercises might prove quite difficult (numbers 8, 9, and 10 perhaps in Chapter 6), all the other exercises in this book will be playable and helpful as players develop many basic skills. The basic bowing exercises will be especially helpful in developing dexterity and improving basic tone.

One great experience I had teaching a lovely amateur lady proved to me that good rhythm can be taught. Before then I had always thought we were "born" with good rhythm and that it would be virtually impossible to teach. However, I was proved joyously wrong! Over a period of at least a year we worked every week with a metronome, and progress seemed so slow that both of us almost gave up, but one week she began playing with a wonderful, natural rhythm, without the metronome. She could even manage the introductory "rhythm" exercise to no 6, Scales. Rather like learning to ride a bike, it happened "suddenly." That year spent playing duplets then triplets again and again, using the concept of allowing rather than trying, focusing on internalizing the rhythms and not physically moving too much, really paid off. I know that experience made her enjoy music-making much more, especially with her string quartet.

In the "How to Practice" section I talk mainly about serious students and professional players, but amateurs can also benefit from these ideas even if they practice many fewer hours than professionals, and, of course, the general ideas on how to physically approach viola playing are pretty universal regardless of standard!

How to Use This Book

Generally, I would recommend working through the Notebook in order first. In sequence, the exercises grow in complexity, from the opening pages on posture to right- and left-hand exercises and ideas, so it is better not to jump in toward the end. If you are an advanced student or a professional player looking for specific exercises, then naturally you can pick and choose whatever you want to work on, but I would still recommend reading through the beginning general sections to get an idea of how best to approach the exercises and gain the most from them.

Although the exercises are essentially sequential, depending on your technical strengths and weaknesses, you can work on them in a different order. For example, if Left-Hand exercise no. 1, "Finger Patterns," proves problematic in terms of extending especially the 4th finger, then you could look at exercise 3a, "Upward Finger Stretches," which utilizes the 4th finger, before going back to "Finger Patterns." The main goal of this book is to contain most, if not all, the material you need to develop a good technique. That being said, we all have different issues and need to be creative in how we fix them. Thus, the material might occasionally work better for you in a different order.

This book is intended to become a basic guide; after working at it over a few months (or longer) with a teacher, or alone, you should find that it is something you can use for daily warm-up routines or to return to at any time later, either to revisit certain exercises or to add new ideas. I also feel these exercises could and should be mixed with exercises by, for example, Sevcik or Schradieck for variety. There is nothing more boring than playing the same things day in and day out.

Before playing any of the exercises, do read through them carefully, taking special note of the instructions. Also, be aware that some exercises have variations attached and different formats.

There are many blank pages and some sheets of blank manuscript (staff) paper that you can use to make notes, write down exercises that you might think of yourself, or jot down ideas you might learn in a master class or lesson—hence the origin of the title "Notebook," as something you can keep for reference and for literally taking notes.

→: this symbol appears in some of the photographs and is intended to point to areas of excessive tension.

⏵ This symbol will lead you to an online video demonstration of the corresponding section.

The Video

The video tracks are not intended to be a "concert" performance of the ideas and exercises; rather, they are short clips or demonstrations similar to those that I would give my students in a normal lesson. Thus they are unedited, recorded in my studio in a relaxed manner, just as if I were giving you, the viewer, a private lesson. Most of the material in the book is covered in the video tracks, but not all. In any lesson there is only a limited time to get ideas across, and students are expected to find and develop their own ideas after having been prompted by the teacher.

The Use of Mirrors

Whenever possible, practice in front of a mirror, ideally two large mirrors placed at right angles to each other. If you stand and play facing the joint where the mirrors meet, you can very easily observe yourself from all forward facing angles without having to move your head. This is very useful for correcting bad posture, observing the level of the viola, checking whether the bow is straight, seeing both hands and arms, etc.

If you don't have a mirror, at least use the camera on your computer or iPad, or, if you have more than one camera, set them up so you can see different views on the screen.

Playing with a Music Stand

Line your feet up so they face the music stand. You should be facing it straight on and not twisting your back, hence maintaining a neutral spine position. Get used to this in practice; indeed, experiment and see how much tension twisting the upper back gives in your playing if your feet are not aligned properly. In concerts, many performers will play facing the audience, then twist their bodies to see the music stand, which is often facing the side of the stage, and thus induce a lot of unwanted physical tension in their bodies.

The Challenge of Playing the Viola

While I hope we can all agree that the viola is the best instrument to play because of its soulful and rich sound, we have to remember that it is too small for the range of pitches it can produce when compared to the violin and cello. Nobody could play a viola that is proportionally the right size—it would be too large and cumbersome under the chin but too small to be played like a cello. We cannot always use the same intensity on the viola that cellists and violinists can. Rather, we have to be more subtle in our approach. As the strings are thicker and heavier than the violin's, we have to be very aware of the weight of the arm and bow on the string; we have to draw the sound and be very efficient in doing so. While we might not always compete in terms of sheer power, in my experience we can create a sound that will carry to the back of a hall by maximizing resonance of tone. This comes through a more relaxed physical approach, by "allowing" rather than "forcing." The last thing we want to do is kill the sound by trying too hard. Thus, everything that follows is an effort to optimally utilize the viola and bow, with the goal of creating a sound that has all the characteristics and personality of the instrument and one that resonates and carries to the back of any concert hall.

I'm always interested in how people come to be violists: are they "pure" bred or did they start on the violin? I did start on the violin around the age of 11, so quite late, and I was lucky to attend a local Saturday morning Music School. When I was 13, I was playing in a little orchestra that consisted of just violins and cellos—no violas! Halfway into our rehearsal, a teacher came in and asked if anyone would like to try the viola in a string quartet as their violist was ill. Everyone pointed at me as I was already 6 feet tall and looked like I would suit the viola so, off I went. I was told what the strings were (I'd never really seen a viola before), where middle C was in the alto clef and before I knew it, I was making my first attempt at an early Mozart quartet (thankfully with a teacher hovering over me). I never really looked back. Although I carried on playing the violin for a couple more years, gradually the viola took over. I loved the sonority and I started playing quartets more seriously, knowing that if ever I took up music as a profession, that was what I would want to do. Little did I know then that 12 years later, my dreams would come true and I would become a professional quartet player for the next 31 years!

How to Practice

Before setting off on the main purpose of this book, I thought it might be worthwhile to lay out some guidelines on how to practice. If you are a serious student looking to advance your technique, the quality of your work is much more important than the number of hours you spend playing. I personally doubt that practicing 8 hours every day is good for one's playing or for one's sanity! Yes, there are many professional players who have been well schooled in this way, but in my experience, if there is no enjoyment in developing one's playing and practicing becomes too much of a chore, then we are missing the point of what we are trying to achieve. However, we are all different, and as I often state in this book, we have to find our own path on this amazing journey: one that suits us individually as we intelligently work toward our goals.

Patience

This can be very hard to achieve—we can all be impatient to reach our goals, but impatience should not hinder good practice. We have to convince ourselves that slow, steady progress through intelligent practice is far more thorough and long lasting. I learned this the hard way. Like many, I loved to "play through" music from beginning to end, obviously having to stop and work at the trickier sections, but I found my progress toward consistency and accuracy was frustratingly slow until I started to focus and work on smaller parts. So, do learn to focus on small sections and build outward from there. If something does not work after a period of time, move on to something else and come back to it later. Think about why it didn't work: it may be that your method of practice was incorrect; it may be that you just needed more time for it to settle in. Don't allow yourself to get frustrated. This can cause a negative mindset, which will certainly not help. Have determination, but be realistic.

A Notebook for Viola Players. Ivo-Jan van der Werff, Oxford University Press. © Oxford University Press 2022.
DOI: 10.1093/oso/9780197619438.003.0002

Efficiency and Mental Focus

I put these 2 categories together as they go hand in hand. Good practice involves the mind more than the physical aspects, as the mind controls what we do. Conversely, the mind can also get in the way once our technique becomes more natural and subconscious. Physically, we could play mindlessly all day, and in many ways this is the easiest part of what we do. However, with good mental focus on what and how we need to practice, our work gains efficiency and we can learn far more in a shorter amount of time. One hour of focused work is far better than 2 hours of "just playing." If ever your mind is not on what you are doing, stop and rest to give your mind a chance to refocus on the task at hand. Mental focus, concentration, and efficiency are the best tools to achieve our aims in viola playing.

Mental Attitude

We are all different, but it is so important for everyone to have a good attitude toward learning the viola. The vast majority of us have experienced genuine frustration when things don't work or go to plan. Of course, natural talent is a big factor, but if something isn't working, the worst we can do is to beat ourselves up about it, creating negativity toward our playing and ourselves. Indeed, there is a direct relationship between anxiety/stress and higher muscle activation/fatigue rates. A calm but active mind is very important for us all to gain the most from our practice.

I remember practicing open strings while the person in the practice room next to me was hurtling through the Tchaikovsky violin concerto. For a while I felt very inadequate, thinking that everyone else was better than I was, until I came to the realization that I had to do what I had to do in order to become the player I wanted to be. Don't worry about others; focus on yourself. We all have different paths to our goals. Some players are fortunate to have a natural technical ability while others have to work at it more. The end result is what matters.

Don't try to do too much at once, plan your practicing, and keep a true mental determination to do what is necessary to improve. Never forget to congratulate yourself when you have mastered something: it might not be perfect yet, but keep in mind how it was before you started working at it. To be a successful and balanced musician, we should recognize and appreciate the good as much as we understand where there is room for improvement.

When I had just left the Royal College of Music I was freelancing in London, fortunate to be playing a lot with the London Philharmonic Orchestra. They offered me a tour to Japan; the only problem was that if I went, I would miss the first 2 sessions with my new teacher, Bruno Giuranna, in Germany. He visited the Hochschule in Detmold every month and I traveled to see him, finding the money to afford it by freelancing in-between visits. I was in a real quandary. I really wanted to go to Japan but knew that I needed some serious work to improve my technique. So I reluctantly turned down the LPO tour, assuming they would never ask me to work for them again, and went to Germany. Giuranna's lessons were all in a class situation, the class made up of around 15 students. We would play, then we would listen to each other. In my first lesson he asked what I wanted to play, I knew I had to bite the bullet and said an open C string! I was so nervous and shaking with anxiety that it was a horrible experience; however, looking back, it was the best thing I ever did. He patiently worked on me, pointing out areas of tension until, about 15 minutes later, heart still pounding, I was producing the best sound I could: deep, sonorous, and even. Luckily, I did play with the LPO again. In fact, some years later, I was sitting with the then-principal viola in a London studio and reminded him of that time. He told me they were so impressed at my turning down a tour to have important lessons that it made them want me even more! There are times we have to make big, important decisions that will benefit our long-term goals. That was definitely one of mine.

Time Management

I advise my students to set a *minimum* (not a maximum) number of hours a day for their practice, taking into account all the other pressures on them, such as academic work and orchestra and chamber rehearsals. Also, I want to make sure they have time off from their playing to relax, exercise, read, listen to music, etc. Depending on your circumstances, this might be 2 to 4 hours, six days a week. This might not seem like much, but if you have practiced your realistic minimum you will feel a sense of achievement, and if you do manage more, it will give you a real boost. Mentally, you will feel far stronger than if you unrealistically set yourself five or six hours daily and don't achieve that amount. The minimum should be a time that is still manageable even if you don't feel 100%. As I have stated before, take a break whenever you feel mentally or physically tired.

Don't feel that your practice has to be in one lump. Physical and mental rest breaks are vital to enable us to keep working efficiently and intelligently. Some may work well for 2 or 3 hours without a break while others might need a break every 30 minutes. It depends on the person and, in my experience, it could feel different every day for no apparent reason. Learn to listen to your body, observe your concentration levels, and adjust accordingly.

The time of day you practice will of course depend on what else you have to do, but if you have a free day, see how much work you can do in the morning. If you get three hours done before lunch, then you know the rest of the day is yours to either do extra practice or relax!

Depending where you are in the level of your viola playing, you might spend more time on technique than repertoire, or you might simply use technical exercises for a warm up. For example, if you are setting yourself four hours of practice and are spending a lot of time setting or resetting your basic technique I would offer these suggestions.

Always start with the right arm, perhaps thinking about some of my suggestions on bow hold, etc., then move to the basic bowing exercises using only open strings, setting the bow and making sure you can create a pure, balanced, resonant, and full tone with smooth bow changes and string crossings. If you're trying these ideas for the first time, they might take 30 to 45 minutes (especially if you are also working on your posture); if the ideas are embedded, 15 to 30 minutes.

Next, I would advise spending a minimum of one hour on various left-hand exercises. Pick a few, not all, of my exercises and rotate every few days. As you get to know them better, you can play more exercises daily, but don't rush the learning process or miss the point of each exercise, even if it appears "easy."

Take some time, which might be included in the one hour, for scales, or you could set aside around 30 minutes separately. You might feel that doing my scale exercise is all you need, in which case practice that daily in different keys; however, I would suggest working through regular scales, major and minor, arpeggios, double stops, etc. in all the keys in order, starting on C. Practice at different tempos and focus on certain scales within a key rather than playing everything. Be intelligent as to what you need to work on and what you should tackle before moving on to the next key.

Then I would allow 30 to 45 minutes for etudes and finally, repertoire. I often advise playing some Bach between etudes and repertoire. Even if you are not specifically studying Bach, playing any movement of one of the cello suites or the violin Sonatas and Partitas requires a purity of sound and technique that the previous hours of technical practice set up nicely. It is also wonderful for the soul!

If your technique is more advanced and you just want a warm-up for your 4 hours of practice, you could focus on specific areas of technique that might be relevant to the pieces you are playing. Whether it be scales, left-hand exercises, or bow exercises, pick and choose what you need, but I would still always start with some open strings to get the body and the instrument singing together, and perhaps some left-hand stretching as well. Remember that as musicians, we are also fine-motor athletes with physically demanding instruments and need to look after our bodies and make sure they are warmed up and in good shape in order to train at the highest level.

Playing music requires plenty of coordination using small and precise muscles for complicated skills in asymmetrical positions.

If you have only a couple of hours to practice, don't try to work at basic technique too much but do strike a good balance of warm-up exercises and repertoire depending on your needs in that particular moment.

Practice Plan

I like to have a plan for my practice. As a student, I used to keep a diary listing the approximate amount of time I would spend on open strings, simple bow exercises, left-hand exercises, scales, etudes, and repertoire. In this way I quickly learned to utilize my time efficiently and gained a lot of satisfaction from looking back over a week's work and seeing my progress as well as hearing it.

Also, if you are playing an exercise with many variations, make a note each day of which ones you have done, and especially the ones you feel you might need to go over again. This can give a real sense of achievement and be good for morale.

Variety

There is nothing more boring and soul destroying than practicing exactly the same thing day in, day out. Although most of what you need technically is in this book, rotate my exercises with the ones by Sevcik, Schradieck, Dounis, and Casorti, or exercises by more contemporary players and teachers such as Helen Callus and Roland Vamos. Look at scale books such as Flesch, Galamian, and Roger Benedict. The general ideas and attitudes I share about playing in this book can be applied to any of these, and by doing this you will keep your mind and your interest in what you are attempting to achieve very much alive.

Fast or Slow?

I have heard many great and wonderful musicians espouse the idea of slow practice. Depending on what we are practicing, then yes, sometimes very slow practice is helpful. We might be thinking about bow control, pure intonation, working on string crossings, continuous vibrato, etc. However, my concern is that if a passage is practiced so slowly that it bears little resemblance to the final product, then all sorts of bad habits/tensions can set in. If you are practicing a tricky fast passage, trying to get it up to tempo, I would rather play a few notes faster than play the whole passage very slowly. I would literally play 3 or 4 notes until they are at a reasonable tempo, then play the next 3 or 4 in the same manner, then put the 2 sections together. This is very focused work but I think it builds up a passage far more quickly and efficiently. We might feel a need to play a passage slowly enough that we can really hear the intonation well, but it might not be so slow. Indeed, I always suggest playing something on the slower side after having played it fast, just to double check the intonation. Especially if you are building dexterity in both the left and right hands, this is a helpful process. If the bowing is also tricky, learn the left-hand passages with simpler bowings, perhaps start slurring 2, 3, 4, 6, or 8 notes to a bow if there aren't too many string crossings.

Like so much in this book, I want to put across the idea of finding your own individual ways of sorting out problems and issues. As teachers, we can shine a light on how to solve them, but ultimately it is up to the individual player to find what works best.

Another idea is that if you are learning a piece for the first time and working on fingerings, don't fall into the trap of working out fingerings at a very slow tempo. You might well find they do not work when you try to speed up the passage. Again, the idea of playing a few notes closer to the final tempo is better than playing the whole piece or passage at a slow tempo that bears little relation to the final one.

I mention later in the shifting exercises that shifting faster and repeating until the shift is in tune can be more helpful than shifting very slowly with tension. Especially on the viola, we need to be able to glide around the finger board with speed, dexterity, and efficiency and not labor to get from one note to the next.

As a general thought: one advantage many violinists have when playing the viola for the first time is that they have the ability to move quickly, having become used to moving quickly on a smaller and lighter instrument. Obviously knowing how to create a sound on the viola is something else entirely, something that they have to learn and adapt to, but, conversely, many who start on the viola often have trouble gaining the natural dexterity violinists have. There are many reasons this may be so. Viola repertoire is a lot smaller and more limited than that of the violin, especially in the more virtuosic compositions. Viola strings are heavier and speak more slowly, so our responses might be slower than had we learned on a smaller instrument. This is a major reason I suggest getting used to moving around the viola, a larger and heavier instrument, with as much freedom and ease as possible and with the least amount of effort—hence, not practicing too slowly and literally getting "bogged" down.

Using a Metronome

The metronome can be our best friend and our worst enemy! We have to be able to play absolutely in time, yet in performance we have to be able to play with complete freedom (though with rhythmic integrity!). The way we practice with a metronome can have a huge impact on our playing. In many of the exercises in this book I suggest using a metronome within a range of tempos, but the type of beat we play to can make a big difference. Most of the time we will put the metronome on a regular beat, and this is an incredibly important thing to do. Whether playing an exercise or a piece of music, we have to understand the rhythm intimately, how each note relates to the next and how to keep rhythmic integrity over a number of bars or phrases. We should always start with the smallest (fastest) beats possible and then work to slower beats. Perhaps a passage could be played to a sixteenth (quaver) note beat, then an eighth (semiquaver) note beat, then a quarter note (crochet) beat, etc. As the beat gets bigger so we find a little more "freedom," but based on a strong rhythmic integrity. However, a regular, clockwork beat seems to me to be very alien to our human psyche! The most "natural" beat for us is a "heart beat" rhythm, in other words, a dotted rhythm. It could be 1 . . 4 1 . . 4 1, or 1 . 3 1 . 3 1, etc. Playing with this type of rhythm can give our music a much more natural feel. Especially when you are learning, for example, the Bach cello suites, these rhythms can add to the sense of phrasing, especially when the beat goes over a bar rather than a single beat. It gets us away from the purely mechanical toward the "natural."

We should always be creative in the way we use the metronome. As an example, practicing a triplet passage over a duplet beat or a quadruplet passage over a triplet beat can be really useful.

(Look at the Preliminary exercise to no 6 "Scales".)

Recording

It is so easy to record ourselves these days and listening back can reveal things that can be hard to discern while playing. Don't just record your repertoire but also the simplest of exercises. Try recording all the exercises as you practice them. Observe if what you heard under the ear as you played them feels the same as listening back from "outside" where we can be more objective, less emotionally attached, and even more critical!

Finally . . .

In my mind, playing is not a linear activity. We don't improve steadily and evenly; we tend to improve in spurts when something finally sinks in. But with steady work, we can experience that moment of illumination on a particular issue, be it technical or musical, when something suddenly works and feels more natural.

Improvement is like a spiral, with the focal point at the top. We start at the bottom, learning the basics of our instrument; this allows us to travel around to the opposite, slightly higher side of the spiral, where we can apply what we have learned to playing a piece of music; then we go around to the technical side again but now slightly higher up; and then on to the other side and upward, with the goal being the top point, where technique and music merge in the complete violist.

Chapter 3

Performance Tips

Managing Anxiety

Performance anxiety is a vast subject and could be a book on its own. I will offer just a few thoughts and ideas on how I have managed throughout my career and how a few of my students have coped.

It is perfectly acceptable to have anxiety—indeed, it would be unusual if you didn't. The issue is how to deal with it. I remember well, as a teenager, playing the 2nd movement of Beethoven's op. 59, no. 1. I was so nervous I literally couldn't play spiccato and had to glue the bow to the string in the upper half in order to move it at all! A truly horrible and depressing experience, but it didn't stop me from carrying on playing, even though at the time I wasn't really considering music as a career. We all have points in our lives when we wonder if what we are doing is what we really want to do. Somehow, I always continued, however nervous or uncomfortable I felt; something deep inside drove me on. When I eventually decided that music and viola playing were what I wanted to pursue, I really began to work hard and put myself constantly in situations that I knew would be stressful but would help build my confidence as a violist.

One of the biggest issues with anxiety is the lack of trust we give our bodies. If we have really worked at something enough that it becomes instinctive and almost subconscious, then we should not allow our minds to get in the way. The classic example is seeing a tricky shift coming up in a performance, a shift we know intimately and have practiced many times. The mind can tell us "oh no, that tricky shift is coming" and in addition, perhaps we also try too hard; what happens—we miss the shift. But if we trusted our bodies to shift to the right note, we heard that note as we shifted, then it would work as it has done so many times in our practice.

I've learned never to "try" but rather to "allow." This has helped me enormously with my own anxiety issues. Whenever we perform, we always want

A Notebook for Viola Players. Ivo-Jan van der Werff, Oxford University Press. © Oxford University Press 2022.
DOI: 10.1093/oso/9780197619438.003.0003

to "try" as hard as possible. For me, this adds undue tension, both mental and physical. By "allowing," we can free ourselves up physically, and I find that the concept of "allowing" gives me a more relaxed mental attitude. However, I can still fall into that trap. Sometimes I might "try" to do something "extra special" in a particular moment; it rarely works! A former student of mine actually wrote the word "allow" at the top of every page and she said it really helped!

(As a side note, I've also learned that during a performance I must never think, "Oh, this is going well"—absolutely fatal!)

One of the main issues is that the only times we can practice with nerves is during a performance. We can never recreate those exact conditions in a practice room, though I have heard of players who might run or exercise just before playing in order to raise the heart rate just as an adrenaline rush can. I know from experience that the more you perform, the more you become comfortable with it; and when there are no concerts to play, for whatever reason, the first few when they begin again can be difficult until we get "in the zone." If you are a student, a big problem is that you can rarely perform one piece multiple times. I was lucky to play many of the great works in the quartet repertoire 10s if not 100s of times. The first few performances could be edgy, but gradually, through repetition and gaining confidence, they became much more comfortable. However, what got me (and the quartet) going in the first attempts was a decent amount of time studying and learning the work, and, of course, playing together every day gave us a sense of unity and mutual support.

When you are a student, it is very important to play in public as much as you can, as long as you have time to go through the learning process, which is so vital for you to feel that inner confidence with any piece, however easy or demanding. I have had quite a few students who suffered badly from nerves but who all had the drive to put themselves on the spot as often as possible, by playing every week in my studio classes, playing as often as possible in our studio recitals, and reaping the benefits later when they were auditioning for graduate schools or jobs. As I mention elsewhere, all my lessons with Bruno Giuranna were in a class situation, with everyone listening in, whether I was playing an open string, an etude, a sonata, or a concerto. To be pulled apart (and occasionally praised!) in public, every time, was such a good lesson in how to deal with nerves and literally get used to being in front of others, especially fellow students who are perhaps the harshest critics of all!

It might help to actually analyze why you get nervous. Is it a lack of confidence in your own abilities, a fear of failing, a fear of what people might think of your playing? As performing musicians, we all have that need and desire to be "loved and appreciated" by an audience even if our main reasons for playing music is to revel in the discovery of what a composer expressed on the page, and a desire to share that feeling with others. We should ask ourselves what story we want the audience to hear, especially if the work is less known (as is so much of our wonderful repertoire on the viola) and might be the audience's first and only time hearing a particular composition. What an amazing privilege to have the undivided attention of a group of people and to be able to share our intimate knowledge of a such a piece! How many professions involve that type of work?

I am convinced most of us are more worried by the fear of the fear. However much I felt my performances suffered from nerves, they were rarely, if ever, as bad as I thought and gradually I came to the realization that I was more scared of the fear itself than the actual performance! It's just that when you are very nervous it's as if a huge spotlight is shining on you for all to see, and there is no hiding place.

One of my students told me she found that really focusing and listening to her own sound helped a lot. After all, isn't this the most important aspect of our playing? It also brings the mind back toward something that is familiar and "safe." Often an adrenaline rush can make our minds go into a spin, so to focus on what we know and understand can help a lot.

Perhaps a change in your mindset, away from yourself to the music instead, might help. We are there to tell a story, and isn't that one of the most natural and wonderful things we can do?

Many of us become even more critical of ourselves during a performance. Rather, we should adopt a mindset of sharing our story and voice, which is, after all, what the audience is there to witness. All the critiquing of ourselves has been done from receiving feedback while practicing, in lessons or classes; now is the time to enjoy ourselves. Remember, the audience is there to support and enjoy a performance and, above all, to see the performer succeed in that endeavor. It can almost seem selfish of performers when you see them focused on themselves rather than sharing the enjoyment and excitement of their music! Even in the case of an audition, where your audience is actually actively critiquing you, the panel is looking for a great musician to add to their orchestra, school, or group, and they would love for you to be that person. The panel *wants* people to succeed in that situation.

Again, there is nothing wrong with feeling nervous. I actually found, especially early in my student and career days, that if I felt nervous well before the concert I was generally all right, but if I didn't, sometimes it could hit me as soon as I stepped onto the concert platform. It's not exactly a pleasant feeling, but I did get used to it until gradually it faded as I became more confident in myself and my abilities as a performer. Interestingly, I have sometimes been more nervous in front of a small audience than a much larger one. With a really big audience it is harder to focus on individual members whereas in a smaller crowd it is easy to pick out those you feel are looking directly at you—the "spotlight" mentioned earlier.

To finish, there are many things we can individually do to cope, and we all have to find what works for us. Meditation, breathing, yoga, just being bullheaded(!) and determined. There is even research showing that physically active musicians have lower music performance anxiety and decreased perceived pain than non-active musicians. Alongside physical activity should be proper nutrition, drinking enough water, and getting enough sleep (often a challenge when on tour!).

For me, there is nothing wrong with doing what we must in order to give of our best, and also there is absolutely nothing wrong with being open about our nerves and talking about them to others. It is critical, especially for students, to "feel" that their mentors and peers are offering this support with open arms and without judgment. Being able to have the willingness to disclose and address performance anxiety and/or physical limitations/ailments early is important to prevent a snowball effect, which can often lead to injury. We musicians can be strange creatures, wanting the glory and admiration of others yet not willing to be open about our own anxieties or even being proactive about doing something to prevent them!

We can think of it this way: nerves are not necessarily nice to have to handle, but they do provide a challenge and can, and should, instill a determination to do better. The day we lose that determination is the day we should give up! Nerves show that we care—about our instrument, about ourselves, about the music we play, and about the impression we give people. These are all very valid and valuable reasons to rise to the challenge of giving the very best of ourselves. Remember that adrenaline gives us an extra boost and is something to be welcomed if utilized and channeled correctly. Adrenaline can add that extra dimension to our performances, giving us the potential to truly excel in our music-making.

Wellness

In this day and age musicians are much more aware of their bodies and minds, and the detrimental effects overplaying can have on them. We can forget that we are essentially athletes, especially athletes of the small muscles in the hands. As such, we have to take care to warm up and not to overstretch or overexert ourselves. The goal is to build the tolerance and resilience of our bodies to stress and injury while improving how well we heal and rebound. When we practice, we always need to be stimulated mentally by having a goal and remembering why we put the hours we do into our playing. We need to learn to listen to our bodies and to regularly stop and rest, because practicing mindlessly for hours a day can result in both physical and mental fatigue. Sadly, there is a common mindset among many musicians that rest or taking breaks is to be frowned on and shows a lack of dedication! Particularly when working at the exercises in this book, if anything aches or is uncomfortable, stop. We have to build up our strength and endurance, just as athletes do. Much of what we do is literally repetition, going over and over something until it is correct more times than it is incorrect. Repetitive strain injury is very common in our field. Even if you feel

OK, it is far better to practice strenuous repetitive passages for a short time each day, to build strength and flexibility, than spend hours on just one day. This is part of what I would call "intelligent practice." Over time, things become easier. Never overdo it and risk causing serious damage to your muscles.

Musicians are not always necessarily "athletic." Although playing is a strenuous physical activity, many musicians have fairly sedentary lives. Play in an orchestra and you spend your life sitting down! However, I feel all musicians should do some form of physical exercise every day; walking, cycling, yoga, stretching, rowing, tai chi, swimming, etc.—anything that gets the body moving and energized. Exercise should ideally be part of any practice routine and, as musicians, we should get rid of the unnecessary fear around strenuous exercise and even lifting weights. Naturally, we all have to be cautious and ensure we are using "proper form," but these activities can help build strength and flexibility into the body and help prevent long-term injury. Essentially, we want to build strength and endurance of the weak muscles that are supportive of our posture and instrument. With good strength/endurance of the surrounding supportive muscles to distribute the physical load or stresses, the tight and stiff muscles and joints that are already overworked from playing won't have to work so hard!

Consider how important breathing is, not just for wind players but for all musicians; exercises that help us breathe more deeply and evenly can only be beneficial. Oxygen is important in creating energy, and aerobic metabolism needs oxygen to break down fuels so that our muscles can use them appropriately.

I had one student who had scoliosis (a lateral curvature of the spine) and thoracic outlet syndrome. Viola playing exacerbated the syndrome to the point that she had compressed nerves in her shoulders and neck, which caused the pain to radiate to her arms. Eventually she had to give up the viola for a while to have physical therapy as well as chiropractic and acupuncture treatments, and she was given lots of exercises, not just to help straighten her back but also to build strength and flexibility in her shoulders, neck, arms, and hands. When it came time to play the viola again, she was given very strict instructions on how much she could play every day. Starting with merely seconds and gradually leading up to a few minutes a day, it took nearly a year for her to get back to where she had been before, but with her amazing determination and a real understanding of her physical issues, I'm pleased to say she eventually managed her graduation recital, playing with more physical freedom (and a better sound) than ever before.

To this end it might be worth avoiding sudden increases in total playing time. When you have auditions, recordings, competitions, recitals, orchestra performances, etc., prepare your schedule well ahead to gradually build up your playing time and/or intensity.

Of course, these physical issues can and will have a detrimental effect on our mental health, especially if we have dedicated years of work toward playing. When you're injured, the mental struggle is just as hard as the physical one. It can feel as though you are overreacting or people won't believe you or you just need to "suck it up." It can also be hard to find a medical professional who understands what's going on. If you are going through an injury, consider the following points:

1. You are your biggest advocate. Don't be afraid to keep seeking answers, asking your doctor questions, and pushing back if it seems as though someone doesn't believe you.
2. Recovery is a long and winding path, and you will sometimes get better and then get worse again. It's important to have patience and trust that things will improve if you stay your course. Unfortunately, you cannot rush that process!
3. You can still develop your musicianship even while you are not playing. Listen to music, go to concerts, read scores, etc.

However, realistic goals and an understanding that we have to go through what we have to go through in order to achieve our aims makes it all worthwhile and can give us the impetus to continue.

I find it fascinating to have observed so many players who appear to have terrible postures but who never suffer any physical pain or discomfort, and others who appear to look balanced and relaxed but are always seeking some kind of physical therapy for tight shoulders or back, neck or wrist pain, etc. I have come to the conclusion that, essentially, many of us do not have "perfect" bodies for what we want to do. Our individual genetics might not lend themselves to the rigors of viola playing, or indeed playing any musical instrument. It doesn't mean we cannot; it means we have to recognize and understand our physical limitations and do all we can to achieve our goals. We also need to recognize whether an ache is dangerous or not. I know if I haven't exercised in a while and then go for a run, my legs will ache for a day or two after. If I keep running daily, gradually those aches fade away as I build strength and stamina. So it is with playing. If you are trying something for the first time you might feel it, but by not overdoing it and practicing in small increments over time, you will get used to using those muscles in that particular way. However, if you have any type of sharp pain, numbness, burning, tingling, or loss of sensation, that could be bad news and you should stop and consider what is going wrong. (Perhaps if you are extending the 4th finger as suggested in exercise 3b, Downward Stretches, an ache after the first time is OK but a sharp pain means you might be overdoing it or not stretching correctly.) Thankfully, there is much more awareness these days of specific muscle injury, and specialist therapeutic help is more readily at hand. Professional orchestras often employ a therapist.

Medical centers increasingly cater to musicians' particular needs. By considering the ideas about posture, bow hold, and left-hand frame, you should develop a more thoughtful and natural approach to playing that is individual and works for you in the most efficient, relaxed, and optimal way.

I feel that a major issue these days is the expectation of "perfect" performance, of playing ever faster and louder and adding to the already high burden of stress, not just to our bodies but also to our emotional and mental states, especially when we perceive ourselves to have failed or not quite come up to scratch so to speak. However, the most important aspect has to be the music. We strive for technical perfection in order to give of ourselves in musical performance. Like any worthwhile endeavor, there is sacrifice, effort, and frustration in achieving our goals, and this takes a lot of mental strength and determination. For some talented players this might be too much, and they decide not to pursue the rigors of the music profession; for others this is what drives them on. Ultimately, we all have to "find" ourselves and our place in the musical world.

I have always suffered some sort of back ache during my time as a violist and spent a lot of money over the years on various physical therapies such as massage, Bowen technique, acupuncture, chiropractic, etc. I am tall, having a slight stoop from a slightly curved upper back and understand that playing for hours at a time can cause issues, but these issues have never stopped me! They are not life threatening (!) and I understand these aches will not cause permanent damage. I remember early performances with my quartet, especially one at the Wigmore Hall playing the long and unbelievably slow movement of Beethoven's op. 132. Toward the end I could hardly keep my viola up and actually lost the feeling in the ends of my fingers. It was rather alarming at the time, but we had been working hard, playing many concerts, and I had a lot of knots in my back and shoulders that needed seeing to. Looking after our bodies can be a bit like getting your car serviced. Every now and then we need a check-up and some maintenance in order to perform to our best! Over the years I have learned to be proactive, not reactive!

Perfection?

I often wonder exactly what we mean by the term "perfection." To become a "perfect" viola player—what exactly does this mean? Perfectionism continues to be a major psychosocial risk factor for musculoskeletal and neuromuscular overuse injuries among performing artists. However, we all strive to have a technique that is as close to perfect as we can manage. But even apart from the physical issues, I have a problem using this term because it can drive us in the wrong direction. What is a perfect sound? What is perfect intonation? What is a perfect interpretation? At the end of this book I describe my greatest musical moment, in a sense, my most "perfect" musical moment. However, none of us in that experience were "perfect." As individual people and players, we certainly were not perfect. Our instruments were not perfect. Had we recorded that interpretation, I'm sure we would not listen back and think it was perfect. But, in the moment, it most definitely was. Perfection to me is a very subjective thing that means the coming together of all the elements involved in a performance in a particular moment. All the physical, emotional, mental, and spiritual elements come together and blend in a special and unique way. We can never force this to happen though we can constantly work to raise our level of performance to the point where it is more likely to happen.

My personal way of thinking is this: rather than consider perfection, I like to consider "imperfection" as this is, to my mind, what gives us our character, depth, and individuality and makes us all unique. I don't necessarily mean imperfection in playing "out of tune" or with a bad sound, but let's think about our actual instruments and bows. They are made of wood that is not perfect, shaped by an individual luthier who knows how to work with and understand the individual nuances of wood. If all wood was the same and all craftsmen were exactly alike, we wouldn't have the huge variety of tone and color that makes our lives so inspiring.

Some might think a particular performance is perfect; others, listening to the same performance, might not be moved at all.

What is perfect intonation? Our skill comes (through processes as described in this book) in adapting and literally "bending" notes slightly to create more or less tension in a chord to emotionally enhance our reading of a work. However, to reach that level of skill requires the hours spent on basic technique for one to have the fine control all great instrumentalists have.

As I have stated earlier, we should celebrate our individuality, but using principles common to us all, work on a technique that can enhance those aspects that make us unique.

This idea of intonation is an interesting one. It came to light in a very significant way for me when, during a quartet rehearsal, we were tuning a series of chords. I happened to be holding a single note through these chord changes. I kept telling the others they were not in tune with me, and however much they tried to tune, it didn't seem right. Out of frustration I started adjusting my pedal, very, very slightly. As soon as I did that everything fell into place. I made very minor adjustments, but suddenly the chords felt whole and resonant. After many years of quartet playing, I realized I had gained that skill of constantly adjusting minutely to what I heard around me, just as my colleagues did. It proved that, at a high level, there is no such thing as "fixed" or "perfect" intonation. We always have to adjust to create the blend of sound we want. How we literally interpret intonation at this level becomes a highly personal thing, linked as it is with a personal or group concept of sound. This is a skill that literally affects the tone of a group and is another factor as to why every group has a personal and individual sound (thankfully!).

Practice Warm-Ups

As stated before, how you work at these exercises depends on what you need at any given time. Obviously, I would recommend looking at all the exercises in this book for basic technical help, but what about general warming-up exercises before practice on repertoire, a rehearsal, or even a concert, especially if you are an advanced student or professional violist? For myself, I always start with open strings just to get the bow feeling smooth, balanced, flexible, and even and to check that my posture is relaxed and working efficiently. I start with Chapter 5, bowing exercise no. 1, "Pure Sustained Tone," then go onto bowing exercise no. 4, "Spiccato/Sautillé." These set me up nicely for some basic left-hand work. Of these, I normally start with (Chapter 6) no. 2 "Rhythmic Trills." I do this at various speeds to check my finger agility, rhythm, and intonation. I then often go to left-hand exercise no. 4c, "Basic Shifting," starting sometimes in 2nd position. This helps with intonation and freedom of movement of the left hand and arm. I always like to play through no. 6c, "Scales" I might well pick the key of the repertoire I want to focus on (and possibly include some arpeggios and double stop scales) then perhaps finish with no. 9, "Shifting in Octaves." This is great for balancing the left hand, freedom of movement up and down the fingerboard, and, naturally, intonation. These few might take 20–30 minutes and cover a lot of specific techniques that we need every time we pick up the viola. If I have extra time and I feel my left hand needs some more vitality and flexibility I look at no. 3a and 3b., "Upward and Downward Finger Stretches." I start fairly slowly but I find it helpful to play them quite fast to add dexterity.

These are only optional ideas; you must find what works best for you: left-hand exercise no. 1 is great for setting the balance of the left hand and for independence of the fingers; perhaps you want more shifting (nos. 5, 11, and 12) or practicing 3rds (nos. 7 and 8) or more octaves (no. 10). As we gain more and more experience in our viola playing we can recognize what we need at any given moment and make our choices that way.

Chapter 4

Posture

Many of the technical problems and faults we viola players encounter can come down to posture—that is, the way we hold ourselves and our instruments. Certain key words describe the attitude and approach we should have: poise, balance, suppleness, weight (as opposed to force), flexibility. There are, of course, many more descriptive words that can be used, but these few give an idea of the general attitude, both physically and mentally, to which we should aspire.

Holding and playing a viola are not exactly the most natural of physical processes, and a lot of tension can arise from bad posture. To this end, we should observe the way we naturally stand. The feet should be slightly apart and flat on the floor, balancing between the heel and ball of the foot. The legs, knees, and hips should be relaxed. The lower back should exhibit the natural curve of the spine, not held straight, not leaning to the left or right, and definitely not twisting to the left. This is a very common fault, especially when playing from a music stand, and it creates a lot of unwanted tension in the middle back. Your feet and body should face the stand directly, not be angled away from it. The shoulders should be down and the neck straight, with the head balanced evenly. Think of elongating the back of your neck and maintain a very slight chin tuck. When we put the viola into position, we should still have this basic, natural posture. The only thing that might change is the position of the head, which might turn slightly to the left and drop fractionally into the chin rest. The only point of contact the viola has with the body is on the collar bone. The purpose of the chin and shoulder rests are purely to fill the gap in order to allow extra support. The left hand also plays a part in supporting the instrument, especially if you choose not to use a shoulder rest. If all is relaxed and released, it is wonderful to feel the vibration, especially of the C string, through the collar bone and into the whole body. Never feel that the viola and bow are separate objects; they should be an extension of us.

A Notebook for Viola Players. Ivo-Jan van der Werff, Oxford University Press. © Oxford University Press 2022.
DOI: 10.1093/oso/9780197619438.003.0004

If sitting, then we must make sure we are balanced. It might help to tilt forward slightly to keep the lower back from collapsing. This can be achieved by tucking the legs under the chair and directly underneath the body, and by using (where possible) a chair that is both high enough and without a backward-tilting seat. Of course, no one has the same body shape or proportions. For some (especially those with shorter legs), sitting with the feet slightly apart and firmly on the ground, with a right angle at the knee joint, might make for greater comfort. This is a very personal thing, but it's one worth spending time experimenting with. Most violists spend the greater part of their lives playing sitting down, so getting this important aspect right can prevent a lot of unnecessary problems, such as collapsing the lower back, tightening the upper back, and lacking overall flexibility.

Regarding the actual position and angle of the viola, I would suggest the following points be taken into account. Essentially, there are two ways of finding the optimum position for the viola. One is to make sure you can reach the tip of the bow easily on the C string with a straight bow. The other way is to hold the left arm in a playing position, without the viola, and experiment with moving it gently to the extreme positions, both left and right. Be aware of the various muscle groups and how they pull. To find a balanced position requires placing the arm in-between the two extremes where the muscles of the upper arm are "in equilibrium." Players with shorter arms might find that the viola needs to be more in front of them to achieve a straight bow. On the whole, the viola will end up at a very approximate angle of 30 degrees from the direction you are facing.

Left arm too far out to the side   *Left arm in balanced position*   *Left arm too far in front*

Essentially, we are all symmetric: we have two eyes, two arms, two legs, etc. The viola is also essentially symmetric, with two F-holes and two strings either side of the central line down the tail piece and fingerboard. It makes sense to me to join one symmetry with the other. The center of the body should join the center of the viola. In other words, the chin should be approximately over the tail piece. This will result in a balanced feeling where we can get from the frog to the tip of the bow with the least amount of effort or strain.

Unsymmetric

Unsymmetric

Symmetric

Regarding the angle of the viola to the ground, I would suggest the following. As viola players, we need to be aware of the pull of gravity. Obviously, this is downward, but to look at many players you would not think so. Violinists, with their smaller and lighter instruments, can hold them higher without the same amount of effort it takes to hold the larger viola. The violinist's left arm is closer to the body. Put your left arm up without the viola and move the hand toward and away from the body as well as up and down. As the hand moves away and up, the effort is exponentially greater. It is better to allow the viola, pivoted between the collarbone and the left hand and with the weight of the head counteracting the weight of the viola, to drop naturally to a position just below the horizontal. The scroll will be very approximately at the same level as your shoulder.

To my mind, this is by far the most efficient and relaxed way to hold the viola and allows you to utilize the weight of the bow arm more effectively, creating a warmer, richer, and more resonant sound. Sound production in relation to the bow will be discussed more fully in Chapter 5.

Optimum posture

Viola too high

Viola too low

Finally, it should be possible to hold the viola easily and comfortably without support from the left hand although, when playing, there will always be an element of counteractive support from the left thumb. The shoulders must be relaxed. The left shoulder should not push up toward the shoulder rest (a very common fault), and the head should support the viola without being forced or pushed down. The neck muscles will then also be relaxed. If this is not possible, then perhaps the combination of chin and shoulder rests needs attention in terms of shape and position. Indeed, it is well worth taking the time and effort to find the best combination of rests, considering that any discomfort here will stay with you every time you play and might well cause technical problems that would otherwise not exist.

A good exercise is to hold the viola on the high side and observe how much you have to push the left shoulder upward to touch the shoulder rest and how you have to drop the head into the chin rest. It is far better to hold the viola slightly lower so the shoulder rest drops into the shoulder and the chin rest tucks in under the jaw.

Many viola players manage perfectly well without a shoulder rest, utilizing the left hand more in terms of support. This can work extremely well and give one a greater sense of freedom, but for some (myself included), shifting downward can be a problem, as the viola tends to feel so much less secure. The extra support required from the head and left hand creates a more complex technical arena to work in. I have noticed that many players who do not use a shoulder rest tend to hold the neck almost in the crook between the thumb and 1st finger, resulting in a much higher thumb which can affect the vibrato as the fingers tend to be more upright. (See chapter 6). Also, without a shoulder rest, the viola tends to be somewhat "flatter," making it harder work to play on the C string (because the right arm has to be higher). However, it can be argued that without a shoulder rest there will be more resonance, because there is less restriction across the lower back of the instrument, which improves the sound. As players, we ultimately have to feel as comfortable as possible with what we do. All players are different, so individuals should experiment to find the optimal position for their own comfort and technical flexibility.

Breathing is something that all players must not neglect. Too many are totally unaware of where they breathe from, often using only the top part of the lungs. Along with raising the shoulders, this literally tightens and deadens any sound we are trying to produce. In fact, if you experiment with raising the shoulders, you will observe a tightness in the chest and the vocal cords, making it much harder to fill the lungs with air. The tightening this leads to in the voice is reflected in the sound we produce on the viola. For a deep, sonorous, and resonant tone, we need our bodies to be relaxed, the chest and lungs to be open, and our breathing to be deep and full.

Another common area of tension is the jaw. How often do we clench our jaws while playing? This clenching tightens the muscles in the neck, which in turn tightens the shoulder muscles. If the jaw and the face in general can be relaxed, we will actually help free up the shoulders and back.

In conclusion, when playing the viola, nothing must be held rigid. Everything must be in balance but be allowed to move naturally. It is perfectly right and proper to move, as long as the movement does not get in the way of the music we are playing or the sounds we are trying to produce.

Right Hand

How do we create a good sound with the bow? There are certain aspects of using the bow that to me are prerequisites. To play an even, sustained tone, the bow should be straight; the pressure of the bow on the string should be constant throughout; the point of contact must remain the same; the bow speed should be even; and the angle of the bow to the string must be constant. Some might think that flattening the hair toward the tip of the bow is necessary to counteract the lessening weight of the stick, or that increasing the speed of the bow toward the frog will make for a better bow change. In fact, due to the nature of the movement of the wrist, there may be a very slight flattening of the hair anyway. The only way to find out is to try these things and decide if they really make a difference or if they just complicate something that is essentially simple.

The following points can help create a balanced, fluid, and powerful bow arm, which will create a clear, resonant tone.

(1) In general, the bow should approach the string from above. This may seem obvious, but many players start the arm movement from below the string level and use more effort than is necessary to get the bow over the string. We need to utilize gravity so that the approach comes from above and is directed downward. I like to use the following analogy: placing the bow on the string can be likened to sitting down on the most comfortable chair. Our bodies move downward (not upward) into the chair. Our whole, totally relaxed body weight is supported by the chair. We can think of the viola as the chair, the strings as the cushioning, and the arm/bow as the body. Sitting takes no effort, just as placing the bow on the string should take no effort. If the viola is held high then placing the bow is rather like climbing up onto a very tall bar stool, which uses much more effort and is not as comfortable! To this end, it is worth considering the general shape of the right arm and hand.

A Notebook for Viola Players. Ivo-Jan van der Werff, Oxford University Press. © Oxford University Press 2022.
DOI: 10.1093/oso/9780197619438.003.0005

(2) Basically, the upper arm, forearm, and bow should be in a plane; that is, the upper arm should be approximately parallel to the bow at all times, regardless of where in the bow you are and on which string. This requires the right shoulder to be flexible and to be the source of the majority of string crossings.

Bow arm position on the C string

Bow arm position on the G string

Bow arm position on the D string

Bow arm position on the A string

Upper arm too high.

Upper arm too low (not parallel to the bow)

(3) When you are resting the bow on the string at the middle, the bow should be very slightly suspended from the wrist, so the bow is below wrist level and the wrist is very slightly rounded.

(4) The fingers must be slightly curved and rest lightly on the stick. The bow should rest between the thumb and string. The index finger adds weight, and the 4th finger takes weight away. For a secure 4th finger, make sure it rests against the ridge just behind the top face of the bow. This means that the stick will be angled slightly away from you. The most natural bow hold can be found by trying the following. Hold up your right arm as if putting the bow in the lower half on the G string (without the viola or bow). Relax the shoulder and wrist so that the hand is "suspended" from the arm. Move the wrist slowly up and down and be aware of where the muscle tension is, then find a natural balance point between the two extremes. Observe the slight curvature of your fingers and the natural gap between them. When you hold your bow, you should still have this general attitude of the fingers. A very common fault is to stretch the index finger away from the 2nd finger (and often the 4th away from the 3rd). Stretch out all the fingers and try bending the wrist and observe how much unwanted tension there is. This tension does not enhance our flexibility or our sound! Now relax the hand and gently close your thumb toward the fingers. You should find that the thumb makes contact somewhere between the 1st and 2nd fingers (this is reflected in the general left-hand shape and position). This is the optimal position of the hand. Always make sure you do not press the thumb into the bow. Any tension here also reduces the flexibility of the wrist. Experiment by moving a pencil with your left hand in to the right and holding it lightly as you would the bow. By slightly tilting the hand toward the index finger (while keeping the same hand shape), any flexing of the fingers should cause the pencil (bow) to move laterally, in the plane of the string. In fact, you may find that to keep the most natural hand shape, those with shorter 4th fingers might naturally pronate less than those with longer 4th fingers. Practice flexing the fingers and see how little effort is required. This is very important in helping to create a smooth bow change. If the hand is too upright on the stick, any movement of the fingers will cause the handle of the bow to move up and down, not in the lateral direction the bow needs to move.

Natural hand position.

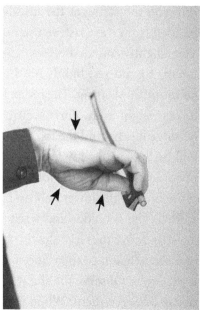

Fingers and hand too flat.

Fingers too upright.

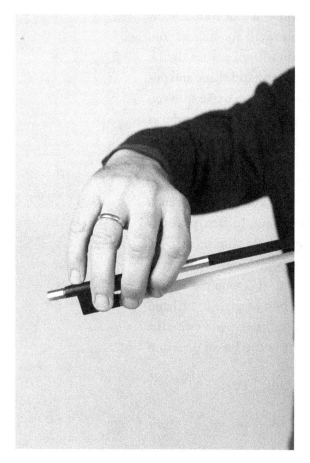

Correct pronation of the hand.

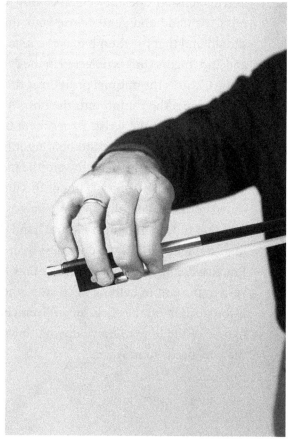

Hand too upright.

(5) Always make sure the thumb is slightly curved and not tight. The amount of curvature is determined by the relative length of your thumb compared to your fingers. Players with shorter thumbs might find their thumbs are almost straight. The curve of the thumb and the curve of the fingers might make a flattened circle. Do not collapse the bottom (first) joint of the index finger, as this will create tension down the upper part of the hand and into the wrist. This joint should always be at or above the level of the stick. If you are not sure, go back to suspending the hand from the arm without the bow, rotate the hand/arm slightly as if holding the bow, and re-observe the general shape of the fingers and knuckles. You will find that when you are playing fortissimo, the flexibility of the knuckle joints may cause the first joint of the index finger to drop slightly. This is perfectly natural. Nothing is fixed; from a relaxed starting point, everything should be flexible and allowed to react to an action.

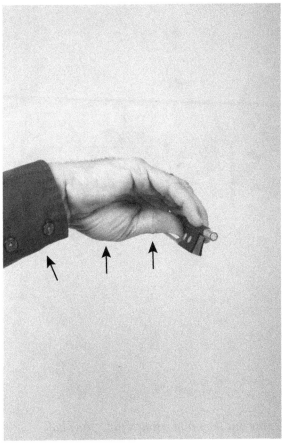

Thumb curved correctly.   *Thumb collapsed*

(6) If your hand has a tendency to collapse, two small things might help. The first is to use a ping pong ball (or something smaller if that is too big to fit), placing it inside the hand as far as is comfortable while holding the bow. This method will prevent the hand from collapsing and also make you aware of how little your fingers need to move to create a smooth bow change. The second idea is to place the thumb underneath the frog rather than resting it on the frog/stick. This might well restrict the movement of the wrist, but it serves to keep the hand open. This latter idea will only be suitable in short bursts due to the restriction of the wrist, but a whole practice session could use the ping pong ball.

Opening out the hand using a ping pong ball.

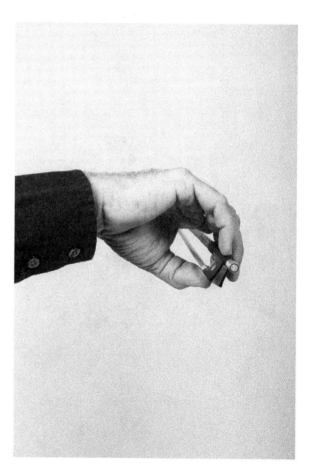

Opening out the hand by placing the thumb underneath the frog.

(7) Once you have found a suitable hand shape, it really does not need to change, regardless of where in the bow you are. If, toward the tip, your fingers and arm seem to stretch too much, then perhaps you should look at the position of the viola. The most important element now becomes the wrist. Essentially, the wrist "leads" the bow, the arm follows, though always parallel to the stick. The angle of the wrist at the tip should be equal and opposite to the angle at the frog, so neither too flat nor too bent. The attitude of the hand on the bow remains the same; only the wrist changes. The fingers will move on bow changes if they are relaxed and flexible. The movement does not need to be instilled; the fingers move through the law of action and reaction, acting rather like shock absorbers countering the change of direction of the bow.

(I often observe players where the elbow leads, especially on the up bow. The problem with this is that if the elbow leads, then the shape of the arm and its attitude to the stick changes and hence the sound changes. Often the cure for this can be found in the index finger. If this is either collapsed or pushed away from the 2nd finger, movement in the wrist is restricted and the "leading" movement is transferred to the elbow.)

Correct hand position at the tip.

Correct position in the middle.

Correct position at the frog.

Incorrect, wrist too high.

Incorrect, wrist too low.

(8) Power comes from the weight of the arm through the hand (mainly via the index finger) and into the stick. Forcing the sound does not work as this kills off the natural resonance of the instrument. By settling downward with both the viola and the bow you can use your natural weight (gravity again) to help create a bigger, more resonant sound with less effort.

(9) A common fault is to move the viola to the right when approaching the frog of the bow. Move only the bow. The viola should be still. If this movement persists, try moving the viola slightly to the left when approaching the frog. This actually has the effect of making the bow feel longer!

Preliminary Bow Exercises

▶1 (1) Rest the middle of the bow on the D or G string. Make sure the upper arm is parallel with the bow and the elbow is neither too high nor too low. The wrist should be very slightly curved downward, with the hand being just below the level of the forearm, thereby "suspending" the bow. Moving only from the shoulder (which should be relaxed downward), keeping the shape of the arm and its relation to the bow constant (in the same plane), and with the bow always at a right angle to the strings, move the bow from one string to the next. Go beyond the C string so the bow hair even touches the wood of the viola, and beyond the A string in a similar manner. Make sure the movement is slow, even, and relaxed, with the shoulder basically acting as a pivot.

Repeat this exercise, but now rest the bow at the tip, and repeat again, now with the bow at the frog. Be aware of any general differences in the movement of the arm.

(2) One thing that is rarely practiced but is vitally important is actually "putting" the bow on the string. The quality of sound we make depends as much (if not more) on our approach to the string as what we do when it is there.

▶2 (a) Stand (or sit) with the viola in position. Swing the bow in a big arc from a resting position (by your side) away from the body (to the right), then up and over the viola so you approach the string from above. In this way you are working with gravity. Settle the bow on any string in the middle. Observe the shape of the arm, wrist, and fingers. If they are incorrect, decide what needs to be changed and go through the motion again. When you are satisfied, with the bow resting on the string, feel the weight of the arm, via the hand (ultimately the index finger), going through the bow. Do not use "force" or tension. The feeling should be like sitting in a very comfortable chair, as explained earlier. Try breathing in; then, on the out breath, let the shoulders drop and settle into a relaxed position, allowing more release of weight into the bow and string. This simple exercise should initially be practiced at the frog, middle, and tip, and then on each string in turn.

When you have done this and feel comfortable, try "walking" up and down the bow in the following manner. Place the bow on the string at the frog and feel relaxed; note the position of the arm. Then raise the bow an inch or two above the string and place it down again but an inch toward the tip. Do this repeatedly until you reach the tip, then, in the same manner, work your way back to the frog. Be aware that as you approach the upper half of the bow, you will feel more counter action from the thumb, supporting increasingly more weight from the arm through the fingers. Make sure you feel the weight of the bow arm through the bow and into the string each time. In this way you will learn to be comfortable, relaxed, and familiar with every part of the bow. When you play whole bows, you should have less tension, more release, and a richer, more fluid sound. ▶ 3

(b) Once you have done this satisfactorily, move on to placing the bow on the string at the frog, releasing it as in a short martelé stroke, and swinging it round in a big arc to repeat the action. Really exaggerate the movement of the bow arm so it literally makes a circle in the air. Do this also at the tip on an up bow. ▶4

(c) Now repeat step (b) but with an increasingly long stroke until a whole bow is used. Next, rather than repeating up or down bows, alternate down, up, down, up, while still moving in an arc at each end, as far as the arm will allow, after the bow leaves the string. Gradually reduce this movement until you are playing normal, whole bows.

Going beyond where we need to is very good practice, as then everything we do on the viola becomes well within our limitations. With the bow, if we can imagine it to be far longer than it actually is—and so any movements associated with it are practiced beyond what we need—we can create a much more comfortable and flexible physical arena in which to work, with far less tension. The following two exercises highlight this idea. Make sure that only the bow moves and not the viola, which should be kept still and relaxed.

(3) Holding the bow normally, play whole bows on each string, but travel beyond the tip (in as straight a line as possible) until the arm is fully extended. Likewise, travel beyond the frog, making sure you stay in the plane of the string you are on. ▶ 5

◉ 6   (4) Holding the bow between the frog and the middle, play whole bows (make sure you play right to the frog).

After practicing in these ways for a while, when returning to bowing normally you should find that the bow feels much shorter and easier to manage.

◉ 7   (5) Before practicing the following section, "Bowing Exercises," try a few whole bows (where possible) on each string, but using only the fingers indicated below (keeping the thumb), the idle fingers being suspended above the stick.

123; 234; 124; 134; 12; 13; 14; 23; 24; 34; 1; 2; 3; 4;

Also, try playing without the support of the thumb. You might need to tilt the stick away from you and make sure the fingers are fully around the stick in order not to drop the bow.

This exercise is incredibly useful for discovering exactly the role each finger or combination of fingers plays. It also develops strength and will lead to absolute security of the fingers on the bow.

Many players suffer from a lack of security of the 4th finger on the stick, due in large part to either a bad hand position or a general lack of contact, especially toward the tip. The latter is not necessarily a bad thing but in general, the more contact, the safer and more secure you will become.

One method I have tried to cure a 4th finger that refuses to have constant contact with the stick is to place a small piece of blue or white tack, tape, or something similarly sticky, between the finger and the bow. This is just an added help and creates a feeling so different that the student becomes much more aware of it.

Of course, there are many players with small hands and short 4th fingers who might not physically be able to keep the 4th finger on the stick all the way to the tip. Every player has to make some compromises and develop their own way of playing due to individual physical characteristics, but I am outlining certain basic ideas that every player should at least consider.

Bowing Exercises

While executing the Bowing Exercises, be equally focused on your left hand as you are on the right hand/arm. Some players might automatically rest their left hand on the shoulder of the viola, but this takes away from the practicality of doing these exercises for a couple of reasons:

1. The left hand is in a playing position the whole time when we are playing a piece of music, so to keep things consistent, the left hand should be in a playing position while doing the bow exercises. That way, any physical tension areas or positional adjustments that need to be made are true to the way one actually plays.
2. The left hand can stabilize the instrument in an unrealistic way if it is resting on the shoulder, and it can cause the viola not to be in the correct playing position—it can become lazy.

If remembering to keep the left hand in a playing position is difficult, you could practice playing simple fingered double stops while trying to maintain a relaxed and free open-string sound. For example, play 4ths instead of open 5ths: start with a D and open G going to an A and open D, etc. It's good for hearing that special resonance with certain intervals and helps build, on a very fundamental level, really good intonation.

Practicing these and similar exercises as a student really gave me a good sense of poise and control in my playing which I like to think enabled my left hand to be more supple and secure. I know that what one hand/arm does is easily reflected in the other. Through them I learned to focus on what was necessary and to eliminate that which wasn't, creating better habits that have stayed with me through my professional career.

1

Pure Sustained Tone

Play this exercise using half bows (both upper and lower), a third of the bow in the middle, and then finally whole bows. Also practice with different points of contact and different rhythms.

Keep the bow straight at all times. The advantage to playing two strings together is that it is very obvious when the bow is not in the plane of both strings. Uneven pressure on either string will cause it to lose resonance and even slightly change pitch.

Repeat each phrase 10, 20, or even more times, until you feel totally at ease with the way the bow is moving and with the sound you are producing. When you repeat it many times, the physical movement becomes instinctive and effortless. You will be aware of only a pure, balanced, and even tone. Generally, what happens is that, initially, one's mind is very focused on the task at hand. You will be aware of everything and trying to correct things that are wrong. After a while, the mind wanders, which is natural and to be expected. The body continues, though, and you may find that minutes later your mind comes back into focus in a more detached fashion. The mind can observe the body doing what is necessary without interfering. It literally "allows" the physical side to work without getting in the way, hence the whole process of creating a smooth, even tone becomes natural. This is very important for all aspects of viola playing, from tone production, to good intonation, to even and accurate shifting. Thus we create a technical basis ready for use as an expressive, musical tool.

With the metronome set at 120, play the first part of the exercise starting with a short, smooth stroke at the frog, 1/8th of a bow per beat. Then 1/4 bow (2 beats), 1/3 bow (3 beats), 1/2 bow (4 beats), etc., all the way to a whole bow (8 beats). Then repeat but now starting on an up bow.

If the bow changes prove awkward, just practice on each pair of strings in turn, then go back to the written exercise.

Play with different dynamics. Either *forte*, *piano*, or *pianissimo*. You can also add crescendos and diminuendos from one bar to the next.

Practice the whole exercise flautando, with a very light bow over the fingerboard.

A common fault in the latter part of this exercise is to overpress on the top two strings. Get used to the idea that less weight is needed than on the bottom two strings for them to speak clearly and with full resonance.

The final two lines of this exercise are really excellent for learning how to play chords. Any of my students who have trouble with, for example, the final chords of the Prelude from Bach's D minor Cello Suite, have benefited hugely from this simple exercise.

Play with double stop harmonics as follows:

2

Martelé Bow Placement

This exercise should be practiced in the following ways.

1) Frog, tip, frog, tip
2) Frog, middle, frog, middle
3) Middle, tip, middle, tip
4) All at the frog
5) All in the middle
6) All at the tip

Each of 1) to 6) should be played with the bowings as indicated in the exercise.

a) down up; b) down down; c) up up; d) up down;

This makes 24 variations in total.

Between notes, your bow should move in a smooth arc.

Never let the bow drop below the level of the strings.

Use a metronome. A good starting point is quarter note (crochet) = 70, but you should be able to go much slower and faster. As your speed increases, the arc will lessen.

Also practice with your eyes shut; this will help heighten muscle memory.

If you have trouble with coordination, start on one string only with 5b, then 5c, then 5a and finally 5d. Then gradually add in other strings, other numbers, etc.

The bow should just grab or pinch the string, then release. It is easy to get lazy with this stroke so keep it very short and sharp. It is more of a touch and release action, not carefully placing the notes.

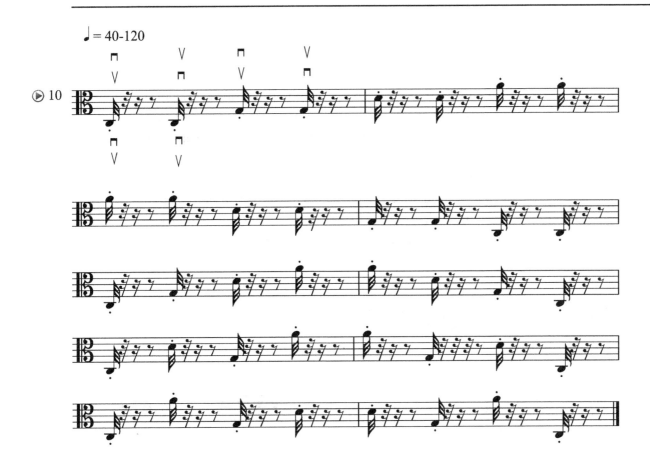

44

3

Smooth Bow Changes

Use the following bow variations either on open strings or on a C major scale.

Make sure that your fingers are loose and flexible and that the hand is turned (pronated) slightly in toward the stick, without collapsing the knuckles, so that any finger movement is in the direction of the bow.

Use a metronome: start at quarter note (crochet) = 40.

Replace the outward physical movements of your body (tapping your foot, bobbing your head, etc.) with the "swing" of the bow in tempo. Feel the rhythm with how you subdivide to evenly use the whole bow.

4A

Spiccato/Sautillé

Play in the middle or just below the middle of the bow, allowing the bow to come off the string slightly. The greater the string crossing, the greater the movement of the right shoulder.

This simple exercise is designed for learning to coordinate the movements of the right fingers, wrist, and arm.

Remember:

1) The upper arm should always be parallel to the bow
2) The hand should be very slightly suspended from the wrist (or you might find you have a straight line from your elbow to your fingers; this is a very personal choice, so find what works best for you).
3) The fingers should be slightly pronated.
4) The fingers should be flexible.
5) Slightly tilt the stick away from you.
6) The string crossings between 2 strings will be initiated more from the wrist and fingers than the arm.

Also play the exercise using triplets.

If any of the string crossings are problematic, try the following. In bar 2, for example, you could play four of each note instead of one (still at sixteenth note (semiquaver) speed), then three then two, then as printed. This essentially slows down the string crossings even though the spiccato stroke remains at the same speed.

You could also start by playing both strings as in a double stop, then gradually separate them. That way you have the smallest motion possible to play two separate strings. It teaches you more efficiency of movement and a realization that too much movement gets in the way.

Space between the notes should be even—equal up and down bows.

Experiment to find the most efficient balance point (basically where you are in the bow) and point of contact.

Another very useful variation is to play *saltando*; rather than down/up, try down/down-up/up.

4B

Spiccato/Martelé

Play this off the string (Spiccato) in the lower half and middle of the bow, and on the string (Martelé) in the upper half.

♩ = 40 – 120

Try with the following variations.

5

Bow Control

These exercises can be hard work on the bow arm.

1) Allow the arm to be as relaxed and loose as possible.
2) The 4th finger has to be secure on the stick, especially in the upper half.
3) Practice using half bows and 1/3 bow in the middle.

Extend the bow past the viola in as straight a line as possible (both up and down).

Keep the bow in one place but do slow, rocking string crossings (remember to keep the bow above the string) even past the string level.

As in the preliminary exercises, try taking certain fingers of the right hand off the stick.

Focus on suspending the wrist and the tilt of the bow.

1) Using whole bows, play silently, letting the bow travel an inch above the string.

♩ = 40-120

2) Using whole bows, play the notes, but allow the bow to travel slowly above the string in the rests.

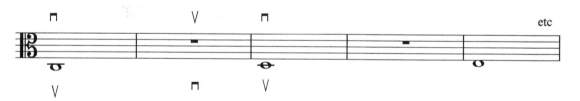

3) As in 1), use whole bows but play silently, above the string.

I have seen much marked improvement among my students over the years through working at these simple but effective bowing exercises. They all help create a balance in the bow arm and a flexibility in the wrist, hand, and fingers. All of this helps, along with the thoughts on posture, toward creating a healthy, pure, and resonant tone and with full control.

Chapter 6

Left Hand

As explained in the introduction, everything we do has to be toward one aim: the creation of a good sound. Before even getting to expressive elements in playing, such as vibrato, you can gain a better sound through a good left-hand frame and good intonation. By "frame" I mean allowing the hand to be in a position where all the fingers can strike the string easily. Don't use the 1st finger and allow the 4th to be up in the air and over to the right of the string. Keep the 4th finger generally over the string. Even more important, don't allow the 3rd and 4th fingers to curl inward while using the 1st and 2nd fingers.

With the left hand, balance is again a key word. Just as your general posture needs to be natural and unforced, so does the position and shape of your left hand. Put your arm in a playing position (without the viola) and try moving the hand backward and forward, rocking on the wrist, as far as it will go to observe where the tension comes and goes. Just as in finding the optimal position of the arm in front of the body, the optimal position of the hand is one where the opposing muscles on the front and back of the forearm are in equilibrium. Thinking of gravity, one would assume that the hand would be least tense in a more upright position. In any other position, one has to "hold" the hand in place through tension. Generally, this might result in a very slight outward curve of the wrist.

A Notebook for Viola Players. Ivo-Jan van der Werff, Oxford University Press. © Oxford University Press 2022.
DOI: 10.1093/oso/9780197619438.003.0006

Optimum position of the wrist. *Wrist too curved outward.* *Wrist too curved inward.*

The height of the hand when holding the viola is dependent on how vertical the fingers are. To create a rich sound, it is better to use the fleshy part of the fingers just behind the tip so the fingers do not land on the fingerboard in too upright a position; hence, the hand should not be too high. The thumb should support the neck of the viola somewhere underneath and the side. Do not grip the neck between the thumb (which should be loose and relaxed) and the base joint of the 1st finger (a common fault) as this will detract from left-hand mobility. This can also create undue tension, which could easily have a detrimental effect on the vibrato.

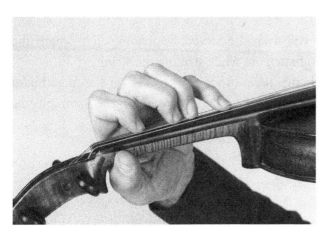
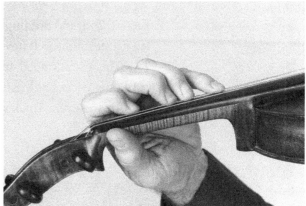

Fingers too vertical. *Fingers in correct position.*

It is very important that the thumb is flexible and does not have a fixed position. For instance, with an upward stretch it might want to move in the opposite direction. But again, thinking of balance, there is an optimal position for the thumb, probably somewhere between the 1st and 2nd fingers. You can experiment by holding the hand in a playing position and moving the thumb backward and forward, noting where the muscle tension lies.

As already stated, the fingers should (ideally) always be in a position where they can strike the string. The hand might need to be turned in more toward the fingerboard so that generally the 4th finger is approximately above the string.

A good exercise is to hold the hand in a playing position and twist the forearm/wrist/hand around in each direction. This is not a natural, everyday movement, so it is worth looking at.

Incorrect, 4th finger too far from the string.

Correct, all fingers over the string.

The 1st, 2nd, and 3rd fingers will always be curved. Depending on its length, the 4th finger might well have to flatten out when striking the string.

There is no need to change the attitude of the hand to the fingerboard until one reaches at least 4th position, and the movement of the hand must be smooth and even. The less unnecessary movement, the better.

1st position.

*4th position, the attitude of the hand
to the fingerboard is the same as in 1st position.*

Many viola players with smaller hands might find it a challenge to comfortably put all four fingers down at once. Some of the left-hand exercises (especially no. 3) will help with this issue. Try balancing the hand from the 2nd finger, extending up to the 4th finger and back to the 1st, rather than extending up toward all the fingers from the 1st.

Another important factor in getting all the fingers down on a string is the position of the arm. Generally, if you bring the left elbow around to the right, the fingers will be more over the string.

The lower the string, the farther the arm needs to come around.

Good intonation (creating a good, resonant tone) is achieved by learning the relationships between the fingers. If one has a different hand shape for each finger or position, this becomes increasingly complicated.

A common fault is to lock the 1st and 2nd fingers together at the lower knuckle. It is very important that each finger can move independently from the lower knuckle and that there is always "daylight" between the fingers.

Vibrato

Perhaps more than any other aspect of playing technique, vibrato can show the soul or personality of a player. Every vibrato is individual and unique. It forms one of the most important expressive tools at our disposal. But, like every other aspect of viola technique, there are certain common principles that relate to every player.

The initial left-hand position is the determining factor that decides the basic vibrato of the player. If, for example, the wrist is pronated to an extreme position either way, then the vibrato becomes tight, the wrist is inflexible, and only an arm vibrato can be used. Many players naturally choose an arm vibrato but even so, for it to work properly, the wrist still needs to be in the correct position.

▶ 14/15/ 16/17   Ideally, a player should be able to utilize both wrist and arm vibrato. On the video recordings are a series of exercises that are much easier to view than to explain in writing.

There are some basic pointers I would like to share. Once the vibrato is working, you have to be able to vary the speed, amplitude, and weight. The weight is most important and is an aspect not all players take into account. For a deep, rich "viola" sound, you need to utilize the weight of the finger on the fingerboard. Putting the finger down is not unlike the feeling of putting the bow on the string, a comfortable and weighty but easy feeling. If you support the shoulder of the viola with your right hand, take away the support of the left thumb and feel the weight of the whole left arm sinking into the string through your fingers. Of course, when playing, we have to use the thumb to support the neck of the viola (rather like the right thumb supports the weight of the arm with the bow), but this feeling of weight and depth will add to the quality of sound you produce.

I find it useful to consider vibrato not just from the initial movement of the arm or wrist, but also from the fingers themselves. The joints that have to be most flexible, regardless of what the arm and wrist do, are the joints just behind each fingertip. If these are held tight, no amount of movement elsewhere will help create a flexible and even vibrato. With your hand in a playing position, get someone to push on that first joint on each finger. If it is tight you need to learn to relax it. If it is flexible, look in a mirror and observe the way your wrist or arm moves. This movement may be very small, but it could be a basis for your general vibrato.

Exercise: One way to free a tight vibrato is to literally trill using vibrato rather than the movement of the fingers. Look at exercise 2 (Rhythmic Trill Patterns) for the left hand later in this chapter. While doing this exercise quite fast and keeping the upper finger close to the string, try playing it by rolling the hand from the wrist to put the upper finger down. If you find it hard to move the wrist, play the exercise in 4th position, starting on a G with the 1st finger on the C string. Make sure the hand is resting against the shoulder of the viola to isolate the wrist from the arm—in other words, so that the arm cannot move. Many players use this type of action for a fast trill. I personally much prefer to move the fingers rather than the hand, as this makes for a cleaner trill, but for this purpose, it is a very useful exercise.

⊙ 19   Exercise: A good vibrato is a rhythmical vibrato. Try varying the number of "vibrato beats" you put into a whole bow. Put a metronome on 40 bpm with one whole bow per beat. Start with two vibrato beats per bow, then four, then six, etc. The movement should initially be large and exaggerated. As the beats increase, the movement should lessen. You can do this on any note and on any finger or, alternatively, you could do this exercise using any scale, either normal three-octave scales or one-octave scales up each string in turn. The one-octave scale is particularly useful as you will learn to vibrate in any position on any string on the viola.

Exercise: If you find it difficult to keep an even and flexible vibrato for a whole bow length or even to get it going initially, try this trick that also works with trills. A slight impulse or kick with the bow can help initiate both trills and vibrato. Play a short stroke near the frog but starting the stroke with a slight accent. You could do little circular motions of down bows. At the same time initiate your vibrato, the idea being that you literally kick start the vibrato. Gradually increase the length of the bow till you can use a whole bow with constant vibrato. Now do the same but starting up bow at the tip. Then try whole bows, down and up but with a little accent, then gradually take away the accent.

Make sure that at all times you are really listening to the sound you are producing. It is very easy to switch off and let things go. We always have to think about the notes, the intonation, the shifts, etc., but never forget that these are only the vehicles to create music. Our tone is THE most important tool we have, and our vibrato has a very big part to play. So always listen and consider what type of vibrato you should be using for a particular passage: how fast, how wide, and how deep. Always support the bow with the left hand; more weight in the bow generally means more weight required in the left hand. In time it should become second nature to allow the hand and arm to do what is necessary to create the "ideal" sound you have in your imagination.

Preliminary Left-Hand Exercise

To be played silently, without the bow

Hold the group of notes at the start of each section and move only the fingers indicated in successive bars. The others should remain on the notes in the opening bar.

If at any time the left hand feels strained, stop and rest before continuing. This exercise is for increasing strength and flexibility. Never force the fingers. If you can't manage some of the patterns, don't worry; with steady practice you will achieve most if not all of them.

These are only a few examples. You should vary the fingerings to create different patterns that will test the strength and agility of the left hand, especially patterns that move from the top to the bottom strings.

If any of the left-hand exercises leave ridges or lines in your fingers, you might well be pressing too hard. See how little tension you need in the fingers to allow them to drop on the strings effortlessly.

Play this exercise in all positions. Especially if you find the stretches too much in 1st position, start in 4th and work your way down. Although 1st position has the greatest challenge in terms of the distance between the fingers, higher positions may require different types of stretches due to a very bent left wrist and the challenge of pushing down strings from higher off the fingerboard.

Left-Hand Exercises
General Comments

The following exercises are designed so that you can concentrate on left-hand issues, though it is very important to be continually mindful of the bow arm in regard to point of contact, bow speed, and weight. All these components must be consistent in order to make the best possible sound and to clearly hear the left-hand intonation. In each exercise, a whole bow at a constant speed is all that is required.

Good intonation can only be learned through repetition. In each exercise, if a note is out of tune, do not move the offending finger. Rather, listen and decide which way the finger needs to move on the repeat and, if it is still incorrect, repeat again. In this way you will learn the exact relationship of one note to another and, when you repeat many times, the memory of that relationship becomes instinctive; muscle memory is activated. Importantly, when a note is in tune for the first time following many times when it was wrong, make sure you repeat it correctly more times than incorrectly. Indeed, if you play out of tune 20 times, play it in tune at least 21 times!

Always keep the metronome on. As we repeat for correction of intonation, don't stop the bow or slow it down. Keep the highest degree of rhythmic integrity at all times (along with a consistent tempo).

With good bow technique and rhythmic sense, you will learn the left-hand exercises more quickly and with less strain. Since they all focus on intonation, first try each relevant exercise (1, 4, 5, 6, 12) without vibrato, to focus on sound and pure pitch. However, if there are tension issues in the left hand, vibrato may be used to help keep the left hand open and loose.

Good intonation is a combination of muscle memory, acute listening, and concentration.

When playing these exercises, be positive and don't fidget! One note starts each exercise; do not play several uneven notes before "really starting" the exercise. That is unnecessary motion and therefore a bad habit. (In a concert you would never play the first note more than once! Get into the habit of finding the first note correctly.)

1

Finger Patterns

This was the very first left-hand exercise I learned from Bruno Giuranna. It is quite simple in concept, but I found it had a profound effect on my notions of good, pure intonation combined with an open resonant tone. It is a wonderful exercise for learning to navigate around each string in all positions.

Always use a whole bow and play with a clear, full sound. It is much easier to hear intonation this way.

Each bar must be repeated at least once, or until it is fluent and in tune. Play more times in tune than out of tune.

If a note is out of tune, do not move the finger to change it; rather, listen to what is wrong and correct it only on the repeat.

Keep a constant hand frame or, in other words, allow the fingers to "hover" over the fingerboard. If this proves difficult (for example, having to move the hand to place the 4th finger), start in a more comfortable position, perhaps 4th, and work down from there. This exercise can be reversed to go upward, so it may help to start in 3rd or 4th position and work up to 5th, making sure the hand is, as far as possible, in a position to put all the fingers down easily. Look at exercise 1c.

When stepping the 1st finger back, do it while you are playing the last finger of the previous pattern so you are prepared and the other fingers haven't moved. Don't raise all the fingers other than the 1st and shift the whole hand back to the new position. If you do, you will lose the exact placement of the other fingers. In fact, you could apply this idea to any finger that is shifting where you can shift that particular finger as you play the last finger of the pattern.

Keep your fingers down for as long as possible.

Put as many fingers down at once as you can. For example, if playing with the fingering 1 3 2 4, as you put the 3rd finger down, make sure the 2nd goes down as well. Likewise, when you put the 4th finger down, put the 3rd down with it. This will help keep a good hand frame and assist in keeping good, precise intonation and increase your knowledge of the relationships between fingers.

This exercise teaches independence of the fingers. Always move only one finger at a time. The others should remain in the same shape and place.

When this exercise can be played with good intonation, try it in the following manner. Play each bar three times: once without vibrato, then with vibrato (still keeping the fingers down), then finally with vibrato but with only one finger down at a time.

This exercise can be practiced using an electronic drone or, better still, by playing an adjacent open string. However, don't overly rely on this as it can make the ear lazy.

I have written out the exercise starting in 5th position but there is no reason not to start much higher if you so wish.

Live in the moment. Looking ahead can sabotage your hand frame (realizing that you're about to move the 2nd finger down, you might accidentally flatten the 4th finger).

If you have trouble with tension between the lower knuckles, do Exercise 3, Finger Stretches first. A neat trick is to use disposable rubber ear plugs. Putting them between your fingers increases awareness of any tension.

Keep momentum with this exercise. Practicing too slowly can actually create tension and overthinking.

Always slide the first finger back but the others should be put down positively.

Another example of being creative in your practice: repeat just 2 notes over and over to learn the exact space between them before moving on. Or when you go to a new hand position and it's out of tune, go back to the last position and practice the movement until the new one is also in tune.

1a

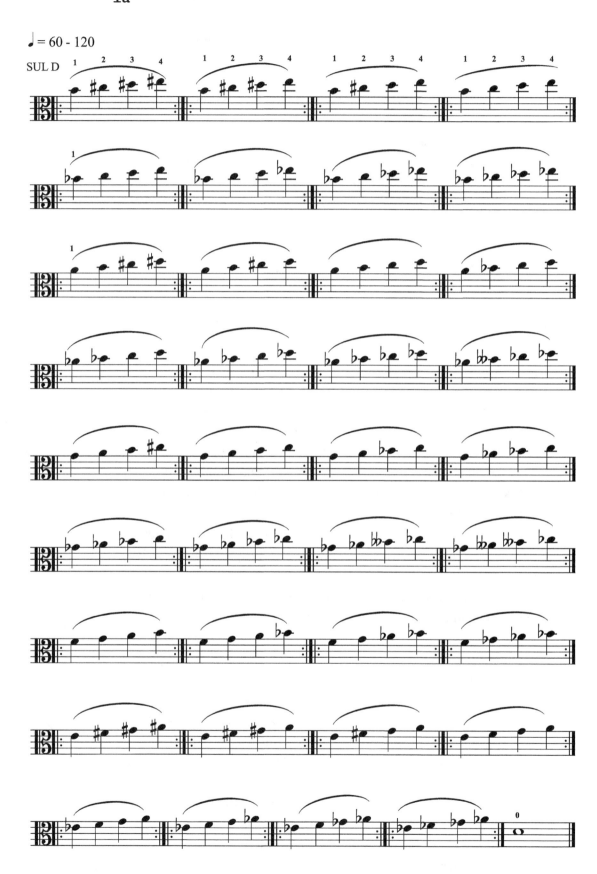

1b

Once you feel comfortable with this exercise try the following variations, 23 in all. You could practice a different variation each day.

sul D

1c

Try all the variations with the following trill pattern.

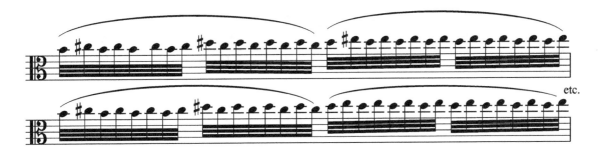

1d

If Exercise 1a is too awkward starting in 5th position, due to the difficulty in putting all four fingers down comfortably, try the following exercise: by reversing Exercise 1a and starting in 4th position, which is generally a more comfortable position for the hand, you can gradually work to higher positions (even beyond 5th), keeping all the fingers above the string at all times. Concentrate on bringing the left arm round as much as is necessary on each string in order to allow the 4th finger to reach the string with ease.

1e

When playing very high on any string it can be tricky to put the 4th finger down, especially if you are playing a slow, melodic line that needs vibrato. To this end, try the following exercise: start in 6th position, going up but only using 3 fingers, first without, then with vibrato. Keep the fingers quite flat, which, without utilizing the 4th finger, should be more easily possible. Do practice this exercise in high positions on each string in turn.

2

Rhythmic Trill Patterns

Always use a whole bow and make sure you play with a good sound, even rhythm, and good intonation.

Keep the fingers down as long as possible.

Start with the metronome on 80. Upon repeating the exercise, move the metronome to 84, then 88, 92, 96, etc. The next day, start at 84, then 88, 92, 96, 100, etc. You will gradually be able to work up to 184 or even faster. Always go back to a slower tempo after your fastest, just to check for intonation, rhythm, and hand frame.

When going speeds over 120, double the length of each bar so you play eight beats of each pattern rather than four.

To assist with a constant hand frame, keep the fingers "hovering" over their place on the string (especially the 4th).

If your hand is very tight and/or you play with very "heavy" fingers, try starting with a more comfortable fast tempo and gradually work your way to a slower tempo as you release and gain more control.

Play a few whole bows on an open string, in tempo, before starting so your bow arm is in the right rhythm to assist your left hand.

Never use vibrato in this exercise (unless using it specifically as suggested in the section on Vibrato). Part of the focus is on the independence and dexterity of the fingers, and vibrating may take away from strengthening this.

2a

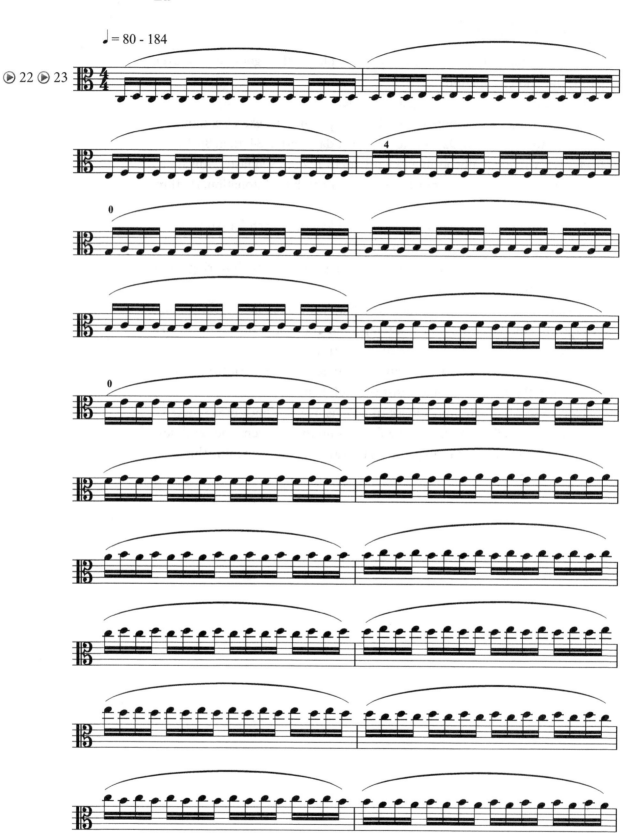

2b

Try this exercise with the following finger patterns. The exercise will not
be in a particular key but you will use the same finger pattern on each string.
When the 4th finger is sharpened or flattened, the next note will be an open
string as normal.

⊙ 24

2c

If a consistent hand frame is hard, especially for those with smaller hands, the following example might help. On the way down, as you start to trill between the 1st finger and the open string, place your 3rd finger on the next string down (hold it silently; do not play a double stop). This will help keep a good hand frame.

etc

2d

If you have smaller hands or are tense and find the hand frame uncomfortable, start in 4th position and work your way successively back to 1st position. This way the stretches are smaller and easier to start with. Still finger 0–1 at the start even though it sounds odd.

etc

etc

2e

This variation is really useful for those who struggle with keeping a regular hand shape/frame across each string. You will find that as the bow moves across each string, the left arm moves in parallel, though obviously the movement is much smaller. As you move from one string to the next, allow the left arm to "rotate" slightly. As you go up, it will rotate to the left; as you come down, to the right. Keep the attitude of the hand and fingers to the string the same, regardless of which string you are on.

This is also useful for those who struggle with keeping a hand frame where all the fingers can strike the string. The last variations using the 4th finger are a big help here.

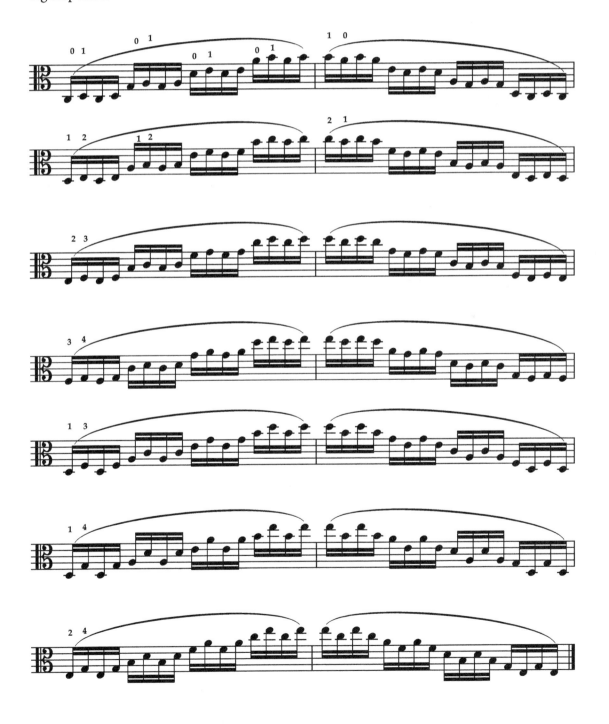

3 Finger Stretches

3a

Upward Finger Stretches

You can play this exercise in reverse by starting at bar 19. On reaching the end, go back to the beginning and play until the end of bar 18.

If the hand is uncomfortable starting in 5th position, start at bar 31 (in 4th position) and practice going up to 5th.

You can also start (or finish) in higher positions such as 6th, 7th, or 8th.

This is a good exercise for opening out the fingers. Always try to move the fingers from the lower knuckle.

Always slide the shifting finger (for example, the 1st finger from bar 2 to 3). Don't lift it. Allow the hand and thumb to follow. In this exercise the shifting finger initiates the motion but you allow the hand and thumb to move with it naturally. If you move the whole hand to shift downward you will lose the placement of the 2nd finger from bar 2 to bar 3.

If the fingers get tired, stop and rest. Gradually, they will become stronger and more agile.

Practice this exercise on each string.

Focus on the upward motion of the fingers as much as the downward motion to keep the rhythm even.

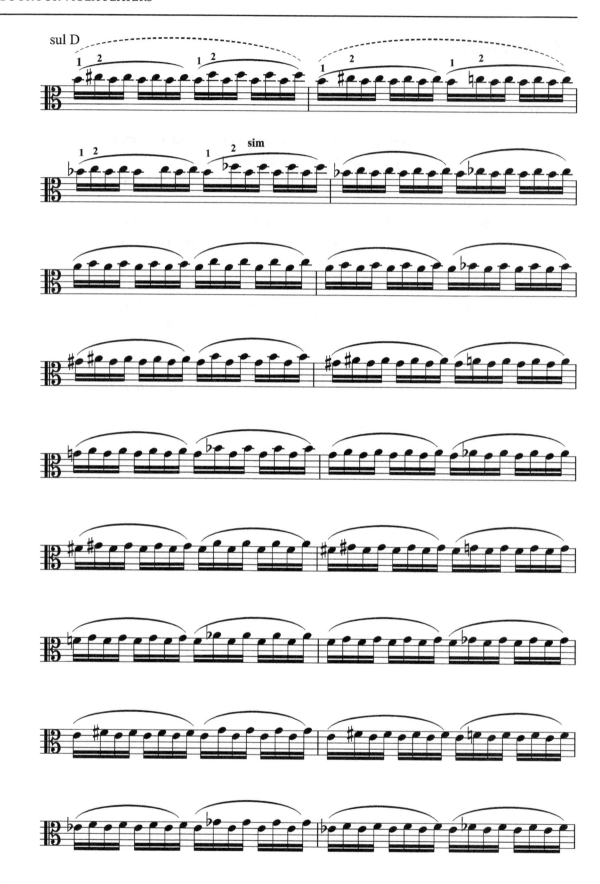

19

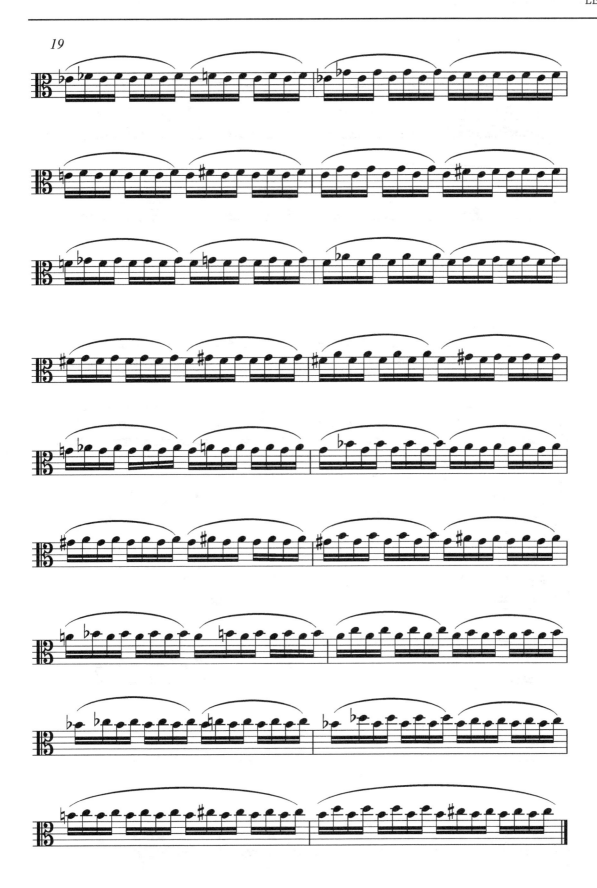

Play this exercise with the following rhythmic patterns.

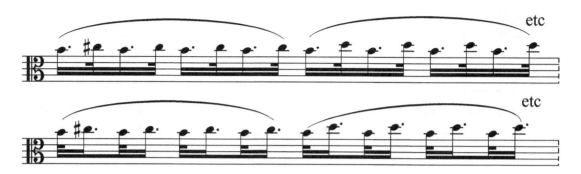

Try this exercise with the following fingerings.

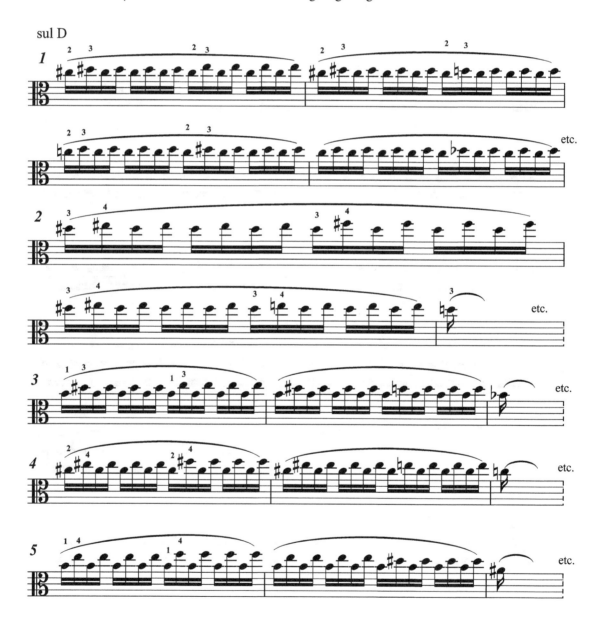

The following is an additional stretch for the 4th finger. As you approach lower positions, the stretch might become too great.

etc.

3b. Downward Finger Stretches

Before playing this particular exercise, put the two fingers you are going to use down on the string and practice sliding the lower finger back and up again. Make sure the movement is from the lower knuckle.

This variation is good for utilizing the additional stretch backward, especially of the 1st finger. Between the 1st and 2nd fingers, make sure the knuckles are slightly separated and not locked together.

As before, practice this on each string.

Try with the following fingerings.

Variation 5 is especially important for opening up the hand and extending the stretch backward. Too often on the viola, players stretch up from the 1st finger and do not utilize the extra stretch back. You can increase your stretch by at least a half step this way. Ultimately, the balance of the hand then rests around the 2nd finger rather than the 1st.

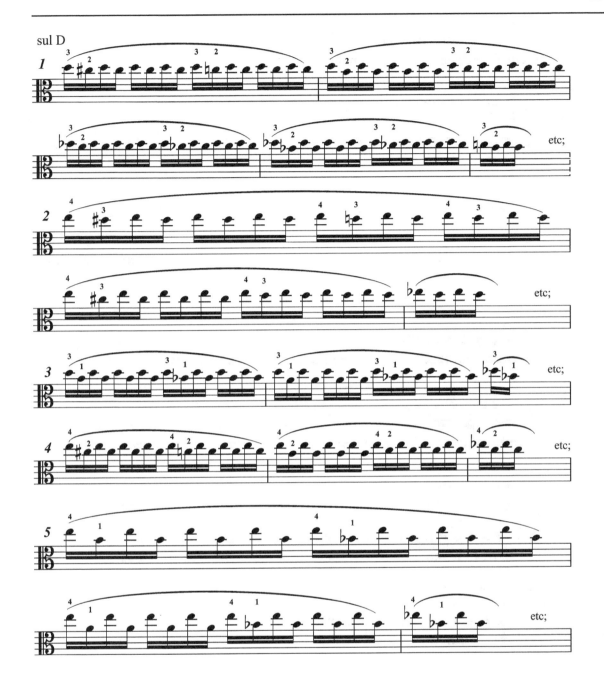

Try the following by silently holding down the diamond shaped notes
while actually playing the sixteenth notes.

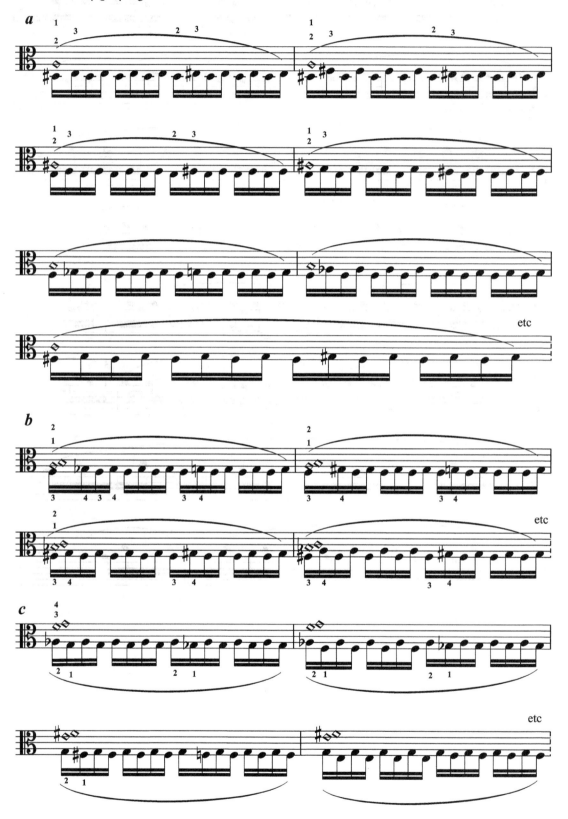

The following variations will extend the hand in different ways. Some might prove a lot harder than others. As ever, do not strain the hand. If it aches, stop and rest.

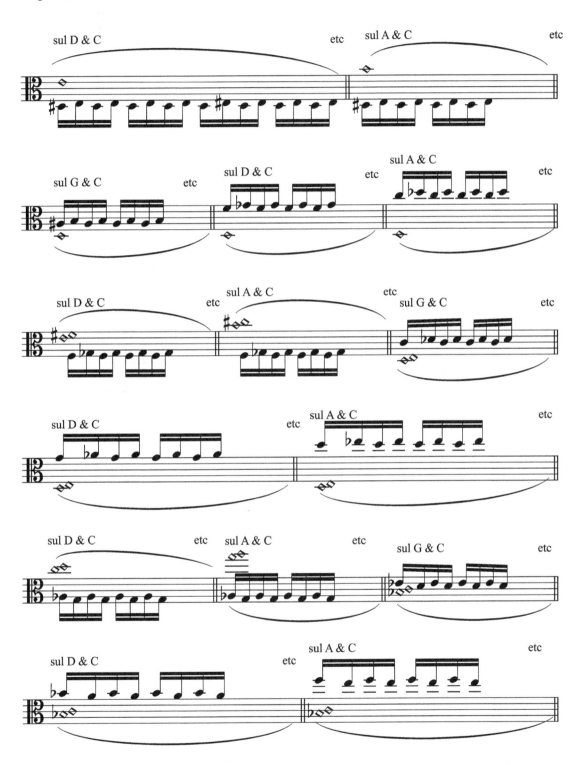

78

4

Basic Shifting

The finger pattern always remains the same; 11 22 33 44 (or reversed).

When shifting, gently release the finger pressure and shift slowly and audibly, keeping the sound smooth until the next note is reached. Make sure that the finger always keeps a gentle contact with the string. However, don't shift too slowly as this can add tension to the hand. Use the idea of momentum. Essentially, momentum is a product of mass and velocity. Imagine you are on a skating rink. You want to arrive at a specific place without shooting past it or having to brake suddenly. With just the correct amount of initial motion you will glide to the exact spot you are aiming for. Momentum in terms of viola playing can be viewed as a product of the weight of the finger on the string and the velocity (speed) of the shift. If the velocity is too great, you will go too far; if not enough, you will never get there! Likewise, if the weight of the finger is too great, you will not get to the next note; if too light, you might overshoot.

I find another useful analogy to be that of breathing. The in breath and out breath are always smooth, fluid, and even, but we can hold our breath in-between, just as we stay on a note we have shifted to until we shift or move to the next note.

Keep all left-hand movements simple. Move the whole arm, not just the finger.

The exercise should be fairly effortless. Glide; don't work to shift up and down.

Make sure, especially on the 1st finger, that your hand is in a good position, i.e., all fingers can easily be put down.

Keep the thumb relaxed and flexible and allow it to travel lightly with the hand.

Hear the note first before shifting, then *allow* your hand to go to that note.

Focus not only on the shift but the next note you place down after the shift (example: when fingering 1–1 2) being in tune. If you find that you are consistently placing the next note out of tune, the problem lies in your hand frame. If this is the case, incorporate exercise #1 into this exercise to further work on your hand frame.

The angle of approach from your finger to the string should be the same, or at least very similar, between 1st and any other position until 5th or 6th. For those with smaller hands, you might find your fingers have to get more upright as you go higher. Don't worry about this, we all have to make adjustments to suit our own unique physicality.

Regarding placement of the thumb in higher positions: every hand is different. Don't overgeneralize or overcomplicate. Place your thumb in whatever way keeps your hand shape and finger angle the most consistent. Those with larger hands might find these shifts possible without having to move the thumb from the neck of the viola; others might need to bring the thumb round as far as the shoulder or even onto the side of the fingerboard. Again, experiment with what works best for you and adjust accordingly.

4a Basic Shifting Preliminary 1

The reason for starting with these two preliminary exercises before the full exercise "proper" is to make sure the shape of the left hand in various positions is correct. Starting in 4th position, with the left hand resting against the shoulder of the viola (generally this offers the optimum hand position from 4th down to 1st), shift downward by moving the left arm from the elbow only and keeping the hand shape constant. The wrist will be essentially straight or very slightly curved away from you. This is an excellent exercise for those who tend to collapse the hand in lower positions. You can check your hand shape in a mirror as you play this exercise.

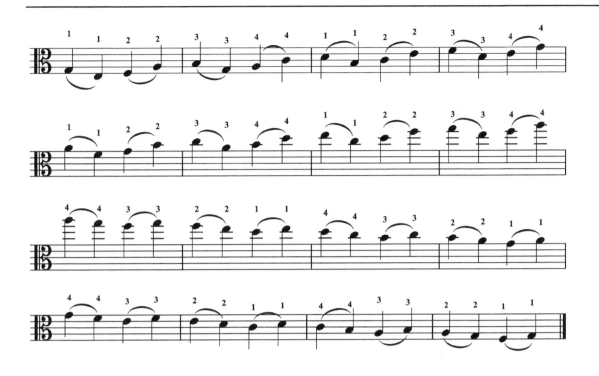

4b Basic Shifting Preliminary 2

Just as bowing can be split into forearm (upper half) and upper arm (lower half) motions, so can shifting be split into two movements. From 1st to 4th position, as highlighted in the previous exercise, the shift is from the elbow; from 4th position up, the movement is generated by the wrist and a bringing round of the left arm. To shift cleanly from a high to a low position you must be able to shift using these two movements, wrist and arm down to 4th position and elbow down to 1st. This exercise is specifically designed to enable the wrist and arm motion.

4c Basic Shifting

Refer to the notes on the previous pages for preliminary shifting.

When you are familiar with this exercise, try playing using different shift patterns. For example, 1st to 2nd up, 1st to 5th down, 1st to 7th up, 1st to 4th down, etc.

Especially when shifting to higher positions, keep in mind the idea of momentum. With too little, the hand will not reach the required position; with too much, it will overshoot it.

Once the hand is moving, it should literally glide to the next position with minimal tension. The initial action should carry the hand to the correct place. As with the idea that one's initial sound is determined by what one does just prior to putting the bow on the string, so a shift can be determined by the initial impulse and the type of tension in the finger.

As stated before, hear the note you are shifting to just prior to the shift and allow your hand to travel to that note with minimal tension.

When shifting down from high positions, especially on the C string, you might find you need a little extra support from the head to keep the left hand free.

Pretend smaller shifts are bigger ones, with the same sense of release and feeling of momentum, to avoid letting the hand get tight.

▶ 27

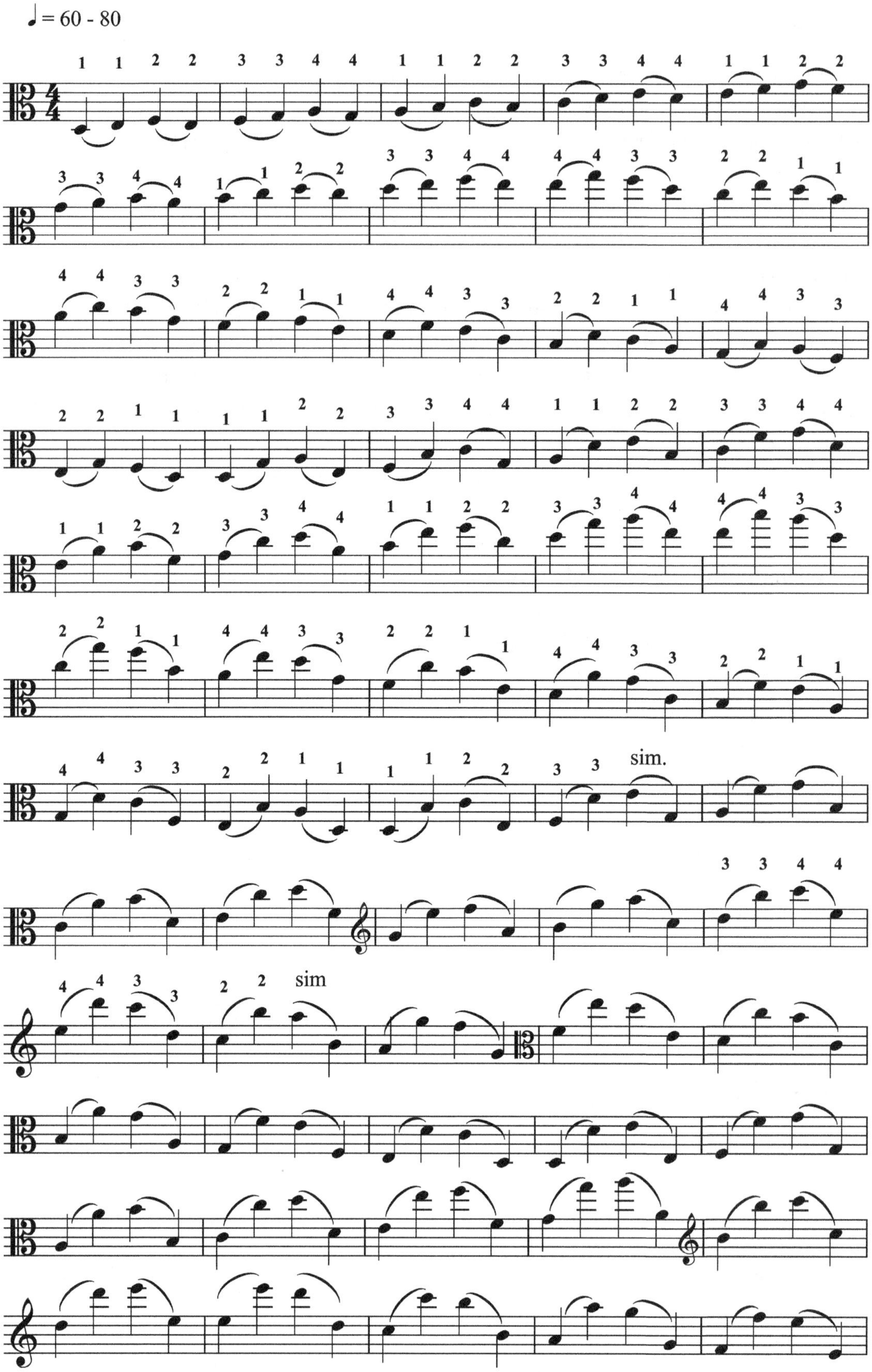

4d

Start on any note as in the following examples.

4e

It would be beneficial to start all the above exercises with the following bow patterns.

5

Shifting

This is a wonderful exercise for freeing up the left arm by playing it faster rather than slower. Rather than focusing on "trying" to slowly shift to the next note, practice with more freedom by playing faster and "allowing" the finger to reach the next note. If it is out of tune, don't correct the actual note but repeat the shift until it is in tune more times than not. Playing faster can release tension that could inhibit the motion of the hand and arm. When you can play at a fast tempo, then practice more slowly but keeping the same freedom and ease.

A rule for shifting highlighted in the variations of this exercise is that when shifting between two fingers, you should generally shift to the new position on the finger you are using at the time, then place the next finger down. For example, when shifting from 1st finger on an A in 1st position to a 2nd finger on a D (as in the 2nd bar at the start of the variations on this exercise), make sure the shift is from A to C<sharp> on the 1st finger before placing the 2nd finger down on the D. In general, you do not necessarily want to hear the shift in this way, but you need not make the shifting note audible. The shift should constitute one fluid motion, from one finger to the next. Still, this process helps in mapping out the fingerboard and gaining security of the left hand.

This is a very good exercise for freeing the movement of the left arm. Although the motion of the arm can be split into forearm (up to 4th position) and wrist plus bringing round the upper arm (above 4th position), like the bow, the overall motion must be fluid and seamless.

Practice this exercise on each string in turn.

Make the arm movement fluid, with as little tension as possible. Shift as slowly and as evenly as the tempo you choose dictates.

Ensure that the upward shifts and the downward shifts are the same speed.

Make sure the wrist is steady, not moving, as you shift up to 4th position.

5a

5b

Try with the following rhythmic variations.

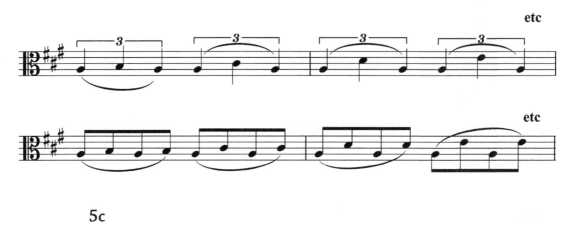

5c

To keep a good hand frame, try the following.

6

Scales

6a Preliminary Rhythmic Exercise in 1st position

Although I always felt my rhythm was pretty good, this scale exercise really improved it, moving from one rhythm to another, seamlessly, was harder at first than I thought. By gaining a deep understanding of how one rhythm relates to another helped me a lot, especially in my quartet playing where, so often, one has to fit different rhythms together in an organic whole, feeling these rhythms not just in terms of absolute precision but also in terms of direction within a phrase.

The actual scale exercise was given to us by Bruno Giuranna, in class, but the preliminary exercise I developed to help just the rhythmical aspect in a simpler exercise.

If you have a problem going from one rhythmic pattern to another, before playing the whole scale exercise, use the following.

Do not "try" to play with the beat by tapping a foot or moving the viola up and down. Invariably, this causes tension, which can actually prevent you from playing with the beat. Rather, relax and "allow" yourself to play in time. This is very important. Whenever we find something difficult, it is easy to tense up. By doing this we actually make the passage even harder. Only feel the beat internally; do not fight it.

Play this exercise and the main scale exercise in the following manner.

Once you are comfortable at 40 bpm, move the metronome to eighth note (quaver) = 80 and repeat. Note that the tempo remains the same, but this time you will have more awkward rhythms of 3, 5, 7, 9, and 11 against 2. This is very useful practice.

Repeat, but now with eighth note (quaver) = 120, so 3 notes (triplets) per beat, then sixteenth notes (semiquaver) = 160 and even quintuplets at 200.

If you have a metronome or app that can emphasize the quarter note (crochet) beat, start this way. Be aware of the strong beats and play to those. As you become increasingly comfortable, allow yourself to become more aware of the subdivided quarter notes and observe how they interact with the rhythm you are playing.

Practice saying the rhythm out loud (with the metronome) before playing it. Focus on just the big beats like you would zone in on one particular conversation in a crowded room. This will help with how you might incorporate your part into rhythmically complicated ensemble works.

Practice smooth string crossings so that they do not interrupt your rhythm.

A common mistake is to make the 5 and 7 rhythms into 6 and 8 where the 6th or 8th note is a gap before the beat. If you are playing perfectly evenly, you will fill the whole beat.

The final goal is to be able to transition seamlessly from one rhythm to another. To this end, also try mixing the rhythms. For example, go from 4 to 7 to 3 to 10, or 1 to 5 to 12 to 9, etc. Try any combination you can. A very common fault is to rush each new rhythm.

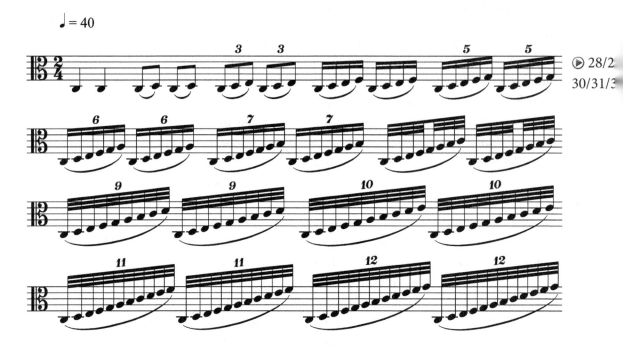

⏵ 28/2
30/31/3

6b Scales

Always use a whole bow; in this way, string crossings will occur in all parts of the bow.

This exercise must be practiced in all keys. It is a really good way of getting to know each scale in turn.

This exercise is valuable for rhythm as well as sound, intonation, and dexterity. Try mixing the rhythmic patterns—for example, going from 1 to 5 to 3 to 11 to 8, etc.

Always shift smoothly, even when playing fast. Do not jump; keep contact with the string at all times.

Play with the metronome at 40 bpm (or 80, 120, 160, or 200 as explained in the Preliminary exercise).

Play totally mechanically, not musically.

Practice without vibrato.

Once you have practiced every scale using this exercise, it is worth taking one rhythmic pattern (2, 3, 4, 5, etc., notes per beat) and going through each scale in turn (C major, C harmonic minor, C melodic minor, D flat major, etc.) without a break in-between them.

No matter how well you play the preliminary exercise, it takes a lot of concentration to go through the whole of this scale exercise without making a mistake somewhere. Make sure that everything, from the bow stroke to the shifting and placement of the fingers, is as relaxed as possible. This will promote seamless rhythmic transitions and smooth string crossings.

From 9 notes per beat upward, it may be worth practicing these at half tempo to start with. As you get more comfortable, gradually increase the metronome speed by small increments until you are back to quarter note (crochet) = 40. Especially when playing 10 or 11 notes per beat, to help with the coordination, put a little accent at the beginning of each bow change. Note that the exercise is designed such that you only change to a new rhythmic pattern when playing the tonic with a down bow on a down beat so some patterns are repeated. Thus 1 note per beat is only played once, 2 notes per beat twice, 3 notes per beat once, 4 notes per beat 4 times, 5 notes per beat 5 times, 6 notes per beat twice etc.

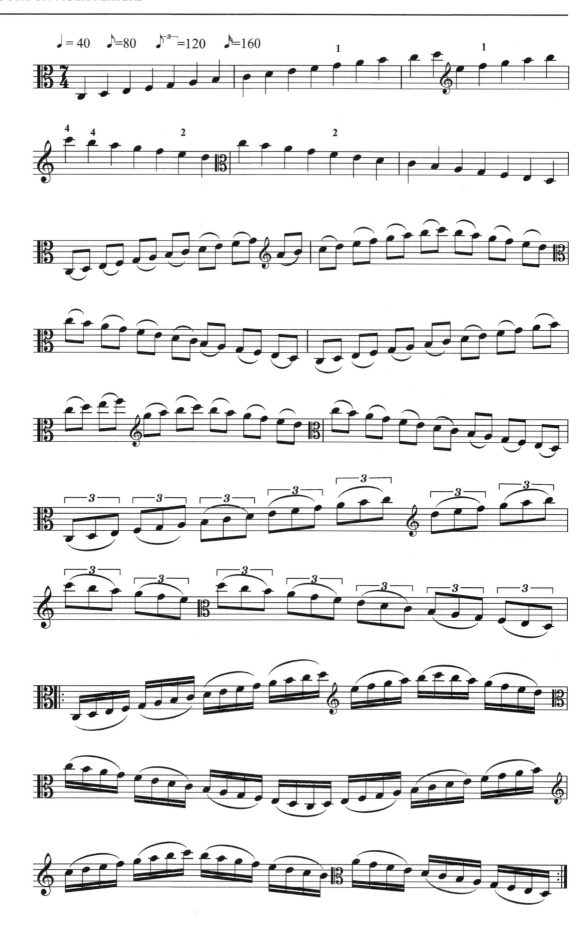

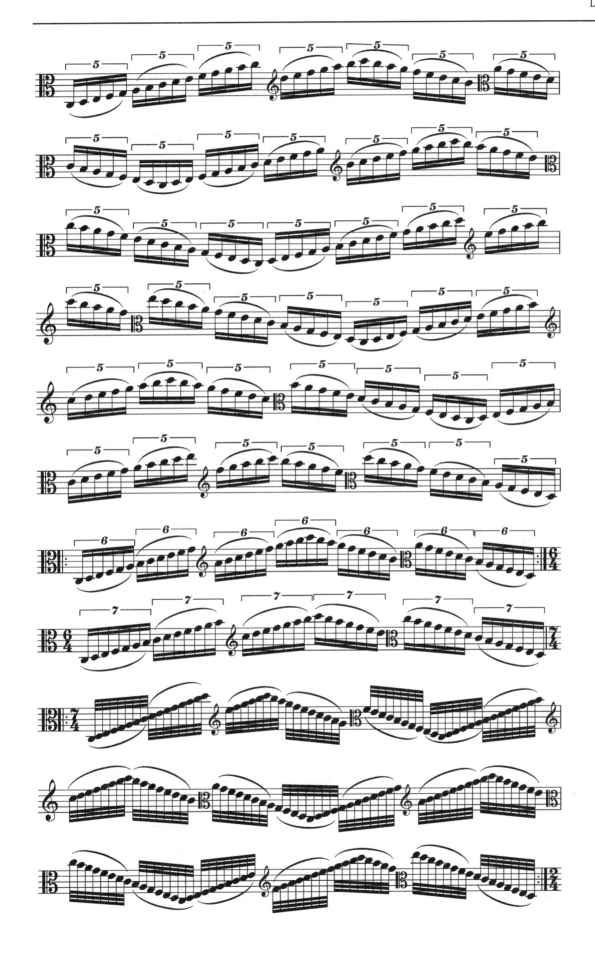

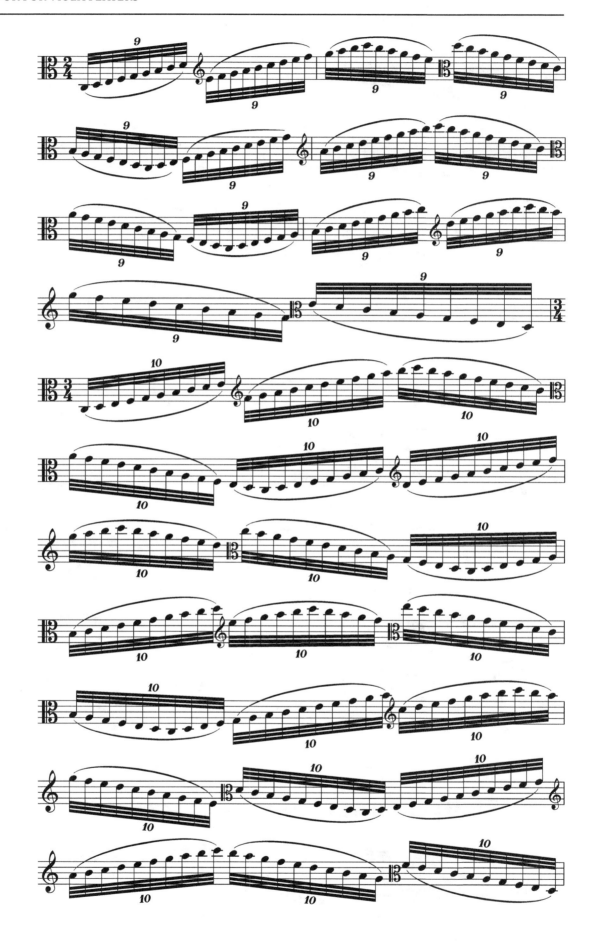

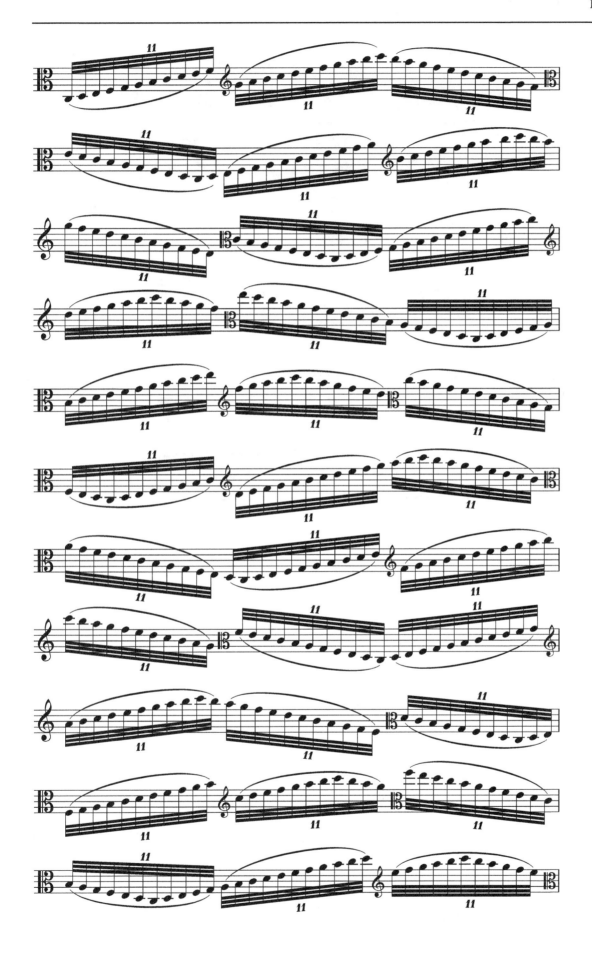

100

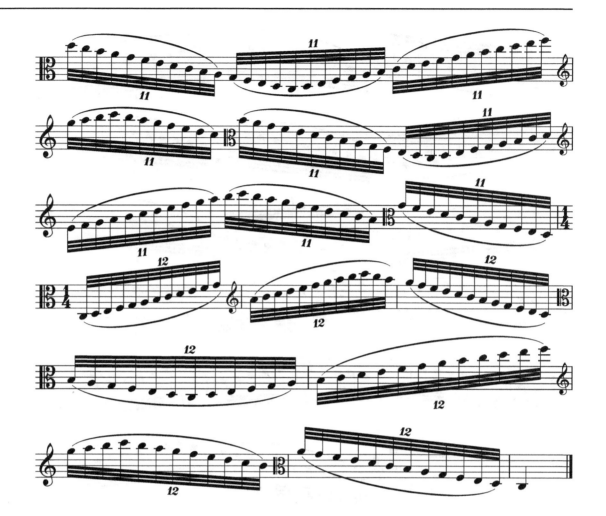

7

Preparatory 3rds

The following double stop exercises are based on exercise 1 and are invaluable in gaining independence of the fingers. By using this exercise in different positions and with different pairs of 3rds, you can essentially build up a scale in 3rds. The following 2 examples show how you can learn 2 pairs of 3rds on the G and D strings as part of a C major scale.

If necessary, use a metronome. A good starting tempo would be quarter note (crochet) = 88.

There are many more rhythmic variations you could make up (for example, adding dotted rhythms), but these should give you an idea of the possibilities.

If, in the first 3 bars, a note is out of tune, do not correct it; go back and repeat the bars until it is in tune. This way you will learn the relation of the fingers accurately. In fact, make sure you do not proceed until the first two bars (which nicely set your hand frame) are in tune.

To master the coordination of this exercise, draw your attention to just one of your fingers at a time.

Break down the exercise and isolate the independence motions as with the preliminary left-hand exercises.

7a

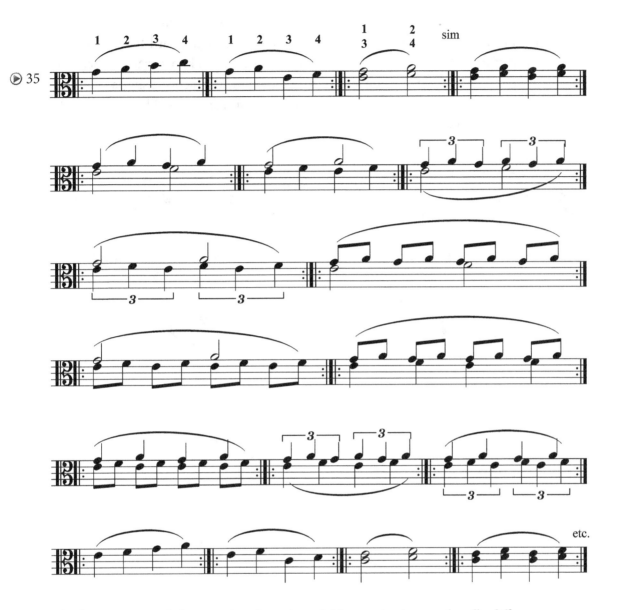

The first time I tried the 2 against 3 version of this exercise it proved really diffi-cult and took me a while, but it did suddenly click—rather like learning to ride a bike. It taught me much about independence of the fingers and helped loosen up my left hand.

7b

One of the ideas behind this exercise is that by practicing each pair of 3rds in this manner, you know exactly where on the fingerboard they lie. Hence, shifting between the pairs becomes easy, because you know exactly where you are going. Another complementary method is to practice using a "shifting" note, as in the following exercise. Make the shifting note audible, just before the bow change.

Also practice the following, which will help establish the 3rds as familiar intervals.

7c

The next exercise is a great way to practice a scale in 3rds (here in C major). Repeat each bar until it is in tune before moving to the next bar. Do not move the fingers if your intonation is poor. Rather, listen to what is wrong and correct on the repeat.

Practice with the indicated bowings.

This concept can be used in any double stop scale be it 3rds, 4ths, 5ths, 6ths, or 8ves.

You can also practice in longer chains as follows:

8

Finger Patterns in 3rds

This exercise has exactly the same finger pattern as exercise 1 but is played in 3rds.

Practice on each pair of strings, ideally starting in 5th position and working down to 1st. If you find it difficult to place all the fingers down in 5th position, start in 4th, working down from there but also reversing the exercise and working back up to 5th position.

You can also play using a little vibrato. This will help keep the hand loose and flexible.

Make sure when changing a note between patterns that only one finger moves. This is especially difficult when moving the 3rd finger down a half step—you might find that the 4th finger goes sharper!

If, at any time, your hand or fingers become tired, stop and rest. Do not strain the hand. Gradually, through using this and the other exercises, your hand will become stronger and more agile.

As a preliminary exercise, you could practice the stepping motion of the left hand without the bow.

Focus on having an intonation anchor and don't be tempted to adjust it. Tune the other notes against this anchor and use it to learn the relationship between the fingers.

As in no 7, you could add dotted rhythms as an extra variation.

sul D & G

This exercise more than any other in this book taught me the meaning of "independence" of the fingers. I found it very hard at first, even though it is exactly the same as exercise 1. But in double stops you can hear even more keenly if a note has moved slightly. For me it was a sudden "revelatory" experience as my brain finally understood exactly what was going on!

9

Shifting in Octaves

Octaves are very good to practice in terms of left-hand frame. By this I mean the general shape of the fingers, hand, and wrist. We should always be in a position to put all the fingers down on the string easily and with the least amount of effort or strain. The 4th finger especially should not be too far away from the string at any time. In playing octaves the hand has to be turned slightly toward the fingerboard by the rotation of the forearm. In fact, this exercise is good practice for getting the hand in the position it should be for most of the other left-hand exercises! Also, when playing octaves, it is difficult not to have the correct position of the wrist. If the wrist is too pronated one way or the other, putting down the 1st and 4th fingers can be almost impossible. So, to this end, make sure your left wrist is either straight or very slighted pronated away from you and definitely don't collapse the wrist toward you. This shape does not need to change until you get above 4th position, when the wrist will need to curve away from you more and you will have to increase the movement of your left arm (think of the elbow) to the right. This is especially true on the lower strings.

Practice on each pair of strings and in all the keys you can, up to a starting point of at least 3rd position.

Shift smoothly, evenly, and with as little tension as possible.

Always keep the thumb relaxed and flexible. Allow the thumb to follow the hand, not the other way round.

When playing octaves, it might help to think of one finger leading and the other following. This way you can focus on the leading note and realize that if a note is out of tune, it will likely be the following note. Try leading with the 4th finger up and the 1st finger down. This concept comes from the notion that it is easier to pull something uphill rather than to push it. Think of pulling your 1st finger up as you shift and lead with your 4th finger then reverse this on the downward shift, leading with the 1st finger "pulling" the 4th finger.

It is very important to play this exercise at different tempos, not just slowly. By using faster tempos, you have to rely more on the left hand "knowing" where to go. Allow the left hand to go to the right place; as you shift, hear the notes you are shifting to in your head and allow the hand to shift there, never forcing it. Slower speeds can lead to a lot of tension, through overpressing and shifting too slowly and heavily. The mind can also create all sorts of tensions, preventing the left hand from working properly. My feeling is that it is better to play faster and repeat until it is in tune, with less tension and greater freedom.

An added exercise would be to name the note and position you are shifting to.

It is imperative that you play this exercise (like all the others!) with an open, relaxed posture and a constant, beautiful sound.

If something is out of tune, do not adjust immediately but instead repeat the passage until it is in tune.

If the motion of the arm is really tight, practice each string separately then add them together.

All of these notes can be applied to the next exercise no 10.

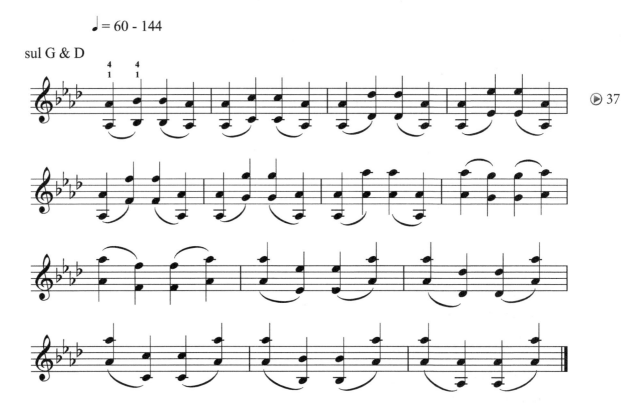

Try this exercise with the following variations.

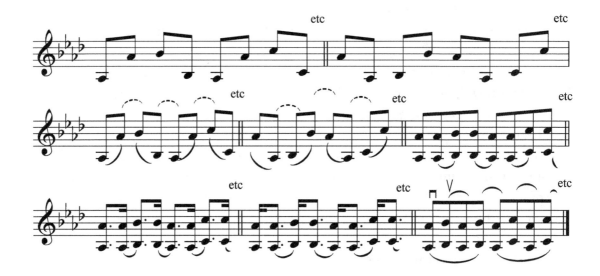

10

Scales and Arpeggios in Octaves

Practice on each pair of strings, starting on any note up to at least 2nd position.

Your left hand should move smoothly and evenly, without too much pressure on the strings. Arm movement must also be fluid and even.

The comments relating to Exercise 9 and the bowing variations also apply here. Also practice these slurred, two or four notes to a bow, to facilitate smooth and even shifts.

sul G & D

▶ 38

You can play the whole of exercise 10 with the following pattern. Keep the left hand fluid and supple. The way to master this type of exercise is through momentum, which is very important in this type of shifting. If the initial impulse to shift is just right, your hand can, and will, glide smoothly to the next notes. Even though this exercise is to be played relatively fast, use an even and slow hand movement with a knowledge of the fingerboard, keeping in mind the idea of allowing the fingers to reach the required notes. Avoid a "staccato" movement in the left hand.

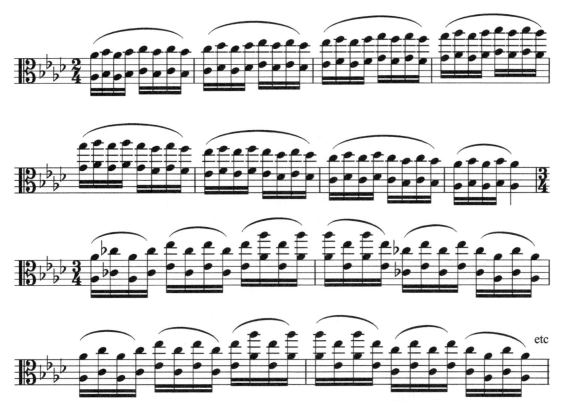

11

Shifting from Open Strings

In previous shifting exercises the emphasis has been on mapping out the fingerboard, learning where a note is in relation to the previous note. The object of this exercise is to learn how to hit the right notes literally out of nowhere—hence the open strings in-between every stopped note. The open string might sound strange in the context of the key you are playing in, but this is also good practice for the ear.

As in other exercises, if something is out of tune, don't adjust the finger. Listen carefully, judge why it is wrong, and repeat until you are satisfied you know where that particular note lies. Remember, each note represents a new position for the left hand. Be aware of what position your hand is in and learn the feel of where your hand is on the neck of the viola.

To really understand where the hand is in relation to the fingerboard, it can help to put more than one finger down. For example, when using the 4th finger, put the 1st or 2nd fingers down as well, and likewise with the 3rd finger. Doing this will help you get a better idea of position.

Make sure all finger movement is from the lowest joint; never put a finger down by rolling the wrist. Keep the fingers alive and energized; regardless of which finger you are using, always keep the others in a position where they can easily reach the string.

Intonation with this exercise can be tricky. Here is a method to help get it more consistent.

1) Take out the open strings in-between the fingered notes and simply shift evenly from one note to the next. Be aware of your hand frame the whole time.
2) Repeat 1), but this time add a slight release of pressure (without the finger leaving the string) between the notes. The finger makes a slight up and down motion.
3) Now incorporate the open string in-between the notes, but with a very fast dotted rhythm, so that there is minimal time when the finger is released from the string.
4) Gradually even out the dotted rhythms until you are doing straight sixteenths (semiquavers). At this point, you are ready to play the exercise as written.

Play each individual exercise on each string.

12

Shifting on the Same Note

Play this exercise on each string.

Your left hand should move smoothly and fluently, moving the whole hand as if changing position. Ideally, the tone remains constant through the change of fingers.

On larger shifts, make sure the whole left arm is loose and relaxed.

Up to 4th position, do not change the shape of the left hand.

Especially when shifting on the 3rd or 4th fingers, you can help keep a good hand frame and secure intonation by shifting with the 1st finger at the same time. Don't hold the 1st and 2nd fingers up in the air. (The second part of exercise no. 5, "Shifting" will help in this respect).

Regardless of how you practice this, your finger should never leave the string. You should, however, practice it in two different ways. First, gliding from one note to the next "slowly," then gliding "quickly." You will encounter both kinds of shifts in your repertoire and this is good preparation.

You could combine this with exercise 11 by adding an open string after each fingered note.

Also practice with vibrato.

sul G

40

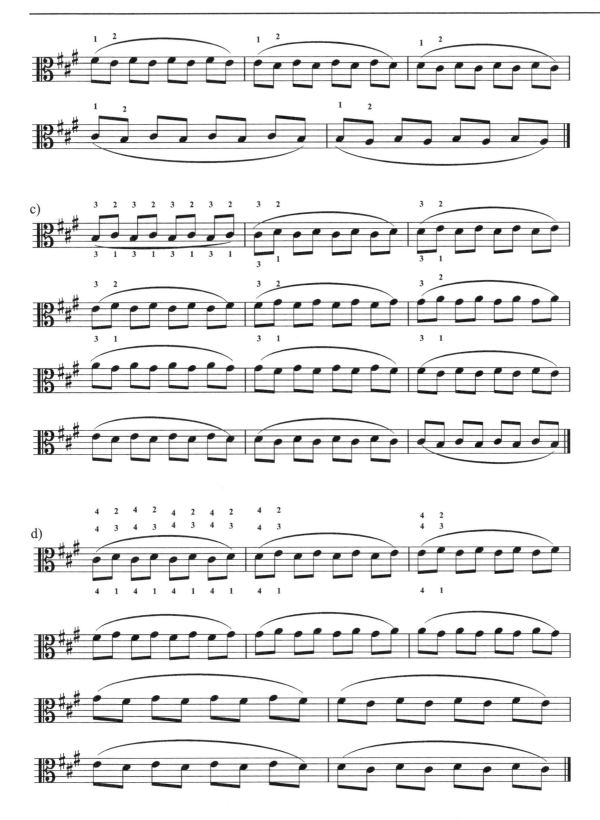

It is perhaps no surprise that 5 of the exercises in this book are based on shifting. To play the viola with real expression requires excellent bow control, excellent intonation, variable and expressive vibrato, and the ability to shift in a huge variety of ways from a clean pure shift to a true, expressive portamento. This final exercise represents a shifting technique I feel is often ignored. Especially when we are playing something very romantic, shifting from one finger to another on the same note can really add something special to a phrase. It is one I encourage all my students to practice.

Chapter 7

Conclusion

Everyone is built differently, and there are many individual ways to approach playing the viola, though based on principles common to us all. For me, the most important and practical aspect is to teach students to become aware of their own issues and how to deal with them intelligently, effectively, and with the right goals in mind.

The following points are the most vital:

- Everything we do on the viola is toward one aim—creating the best possible sound.
- To this end, you must play the viola using "natural" positions.
- Good sound is not achieved with just the bow but also through good intonation. This is achieved through repetition, not by adjusting the offending finger and moving on.
- Don't let the mind get in the way too much. Once you have gone through the learning process, your body "knows" what to do. Therefore, learn to trust your body to do the right thing. The mind can induce uncertainty and doubt. Have trust and faith in your own physical ability.
- Use the concept of "allowing" rather than "trying." This will help both physically and mentally in reducing unwanted tension.
- All bow changes should be smooth and even.
- Don't rush shifts or string crossings; there is always more time than you imagine. There is a fine balance between having relaxed momentum and not using more movement than absolutely necessary.
- It is better to do an exercise with the correct technique or principle and get the "wrong result" than to use the wrong technique and get what seems the "right result" (for example: playing decent spiccato with a tight arm versus slowly fixing an uneven spiccato with a relaxed arm).
- Be creative in your practice: add variations, fingerings, rhythms, different keys, etc., to further the exercises based on your own body, needs, and habits. Use the Notebook as a reference of initial ideas from which you can tailor your own personal practice regime.

A Notebook for Viola Players. Ivo-Jan van der Werff, Oxford University Press. © Oxford University Press 2022.
DOI: 10.1093/oso/9780197619438.003.0007

- If there is a movement you are doing without any real reason (be it a larger body movement or something smaller in your hands or fingers), it is a habit, not a necessity. Habits without purpose should be eliminated.

Once you have a secure enough technique, then you can really explore the emotional nature of music through an intelligent and intuitive grasp of sound and color, utilizing the bow as a singer might utilize the voice, and allowing your viola to reveal its true, expressive character.

What Is This All For?

To play an instrument to the highest level requires hours and hours of practice, a serious dedication to the end goal, patience, drive, ambition, and of course, talent!

All who succeed have a good combination of these things but everyone has a different balance. I have seen many amazingly talented players who don't succeed because they lack the drive or dedication. Talent perhaps makes up only 50% of what we really need.

Why do we put ourselves through the pain, stress, inner conflicts, uncertainties, etc.? Well, the goals are almost indescribable. Playing a piece of music to the highest level, with musical maturity and integrity, secure technique; telling a story through sound; inspiring an audience: these are things that make all the effort worthwhile. My hope is that most professional musicians will have had some career defining experiences that make everything worth it. It might be a solo concert or an experience playing in an orchestra or quartet. I will share three that have stayed with me.

The first was playing with the London Philharmonic Orchestra at the Edinburgh Festival, Brahms 1st Symphony conducted by Klaus Tennstedt, shortly after I had graduated from the Royal College of Music. I was sitting at the back of the violas, directly in front of the trombones. It was a great and compelling musical experience, naturally, but what struck me most, and became a defining experience, was hearing the 3 trombones coming in together on a chord with such precision, perfect intonation, and articulation. It literally sent shivers down my spine. I regularly mention that experience to my students because, as string players, we can learn so much from our brass colleagues in how to start a note. What type of consonant sound do we want, a "buh," a puh, a "wuh," a "kuh," a "tuh" etc.? How do we breathe and move before making that sound? There is so much to consider when we put the bow on the string. That experience totally transformed and informed my attitude toward starting notes.

My all-time "best" and by far the most profound musical experience I have ever had came about 7 or 8 years later, funnily enough, not in a concert but during a rehearsal! My quartet was learning the Cavatina from Beethoven's op. 130. It was not going well. Intonation seemed off, the sound was wrong, we couldn't get the flow right—all in all, a very frustrating time. In the end, our second violinist requested (quite sharply!) that we stop arguing and just try to play it through, so, we did. As soon as we put bow to string, we knew something uniquely special was happening; everything suddenly seemed to work. The sound was incredible, the pacing was perfect. Our playing was of course "in time" yet it had that timeless perception we can get when we are lifted out of ourselves. Phrases transitioned seamlessly one into the other. We felt the most pure and refined of human emotions, the ones we spend our musical lives striving to reach. We hardly dared look at each other as we played, or even breathe, not wanting to destroy this amazing experience. At the end we just got up, put our instruments in their cases and left, without a word. We all knew we had experienced a unique and deeply profound moment on our musical journey together, something intimately special in those few short minutes, sharing something that still gives me shivers when I think about it. In a quartet, of course, our personalities can make life difficult at times(!), but an experience like that truly bonds a group together for life.

My last thought concerns a concert with my quartet at the Queen Elizabeth Hall in London, playing Smetana String Quartet, No. 1, "From My Life." Toward the end of the slow movement, the very beautiful, but wonderfully simple, theme is played by the cello while the viola holds on to a long A<flat> pedal covering 5 bars. I was completely mesmerized by the amazing and glorious sound of our cellist and gripped by the emotional nature of the music. I literally disappeared into my own mind and imagination, transported somewhere else. What seemed like an age later I came down to earth with a bump, not having a clue where I was, until I opened my eyes, looked up, saw a full concert hall and had a slight panic! Luckily my body knew exactly when to move from the long A<flat> to the G, because I certainly didn't! All this happened in a matter of a few seconds but, like any great experience, time takes a very different meaning when we "leave" our physical bodies and experience the sublime!

I truly believe that even one experience like any of these in a lifetime of music-making makes all the hard work worth it, and the wonderful thing is that we can never predict when this might happen. It could be tomorrow or in 10 years' time, but the magic of what we do is always present in some form or other, waiting for us to experience that ultimate musical moment when all comes together, and all based on the strong technical and foundational work we put in as students.

Afterword

I owe such a debt of gratitude to my former teachers, Brian Masters of the Macnaghton Quartet, Margaret Major of the Aeolian Quartet, Peter Shidlof of the Amadeus Quartet, and perhaps the greatest influence of all, Bruno Giuranna. Especially without Bruno, I would not have developed the viola technique and general knowledge, not just of viola playing itself, but of the beautifully and intelligently structured, honest, and unegotistical approach to music-making that he imparted, and perhaps then I would not have had the opportunities to experience what I have been so lucky to experience on my lifetime's musical journey.

Index

allow 2, 7, 14, 15, 23, 25, 36, 48, 50, 55, 56, 59, 62, 67, 69, 79, 85, 93, 109,
angle 24, 25, 27, 33, 35, 80
anxiety vii, 8, 9, 14, 17
arm
    left 24, 25, 53, 54, 62, 67, 80, 82, 89, 109, 121,
    right 2, 10, 26, 27, 29
    upper 24, 28, 35, 45, 82, 89
arpeggios 10, 22, 112
attitude 8, 15, 23, 29, 33, 52, 67, 125

back 5, 18, 19, 20, 23, 24, 26
balance 2, 10, 22, 23, 26, 29, 45, 49, 50, 51, 74, 124
balance point 29, 45
bow 1, 2, 5, 10, 11, 20, 22, 23, 24, 25, 27, 28, 29, 31, 32, 33, 35, 36, 37, 40, 42, 44, 45, 47, 48, 55, 58, 124, 125
    arm 25, 27, 28, 36, 48, 49, 58, 63
    changes 10, 33, 40, 44, 124
    control 11, 48, 122
    frog 24, 27, 32, 33, 34, 35, 36, 37, 40, 42, 55
    hold 1, 10, 20, 29,
breathing 16, 18, 26, 36, 79

chin rest 23, 26
concentration 8, 9, 58, 95
contact 23, 27, 29, 37, 40, 45, 58, 79, 95

dexterity 2, 3, 11, 12, 22, 63, 95

efficiency 8, 12, 45
elbow 33, 35, 45, 53, 80, 82, 109

finger
    1st 26, 50, 51, 54, 59, 66, 69, 74, 79, 89, 109, 121

2nd 2, 29, 33, 53, 59, 69, 74, 89, 121
3rd 2, 59, 66, 106, 114
4th 4, 19, 29, 37, 48, 50, 52, 53, 59, 62, 65, 67, 73, 106, 109, 114
fingers
    left hand 1, 2, 22, 26, 50, 51, 52, 53, 54, 56, 59, 62, 63, 67, 69, 74, 79, 89, 95, 102, 105, 106, 109, 113, 114, 121, 124
    right hand 20, 29, 30, 31, 32, 33, 35, 36, 37, 44, 45, 48
fingerboard 2, 22, 24, 40, 51, 52, 53, 56, 59, 79, 89, 104, 109, 113, 114
flexibility 18, 22, 23, 24, 26, 29, 31, 49, 56
forearm
    left 50, 52, 89, 109
    right 28, 35

gravity 25, 27, 35, 50

hand frame 20, 59, 63, 66, 67, 79, 92, 102, 109, 114, 121

intonation 2, 11, 20, 21, 22, 38, 40, 50, 53, 55, 58, 59, 63, 95, 105, 106, 114, 121, 124
intonation anchor 106

jaw 26

knuckle(s) 31, 44, 53, 59, 69, 74

martele 36, 42, 47
metronome 3, 12, 13, 58
momentum 59, 79, 85, 113, 124
muscle memory 42, 58

neck 18, 19, 23, 25, 26
neck (of the viola) 26, 51, 53, 79, 114
nerves 15, 16, 17

134

pain 17, 18, 19, 125
performance anxiety 14, 17
point of contact 23, 27, 45, 58
position (postural) 1, 5, 23, 24, 25, 26, 28,
    29, 30, 33, 34, 35, 36, 37, 38, 50, 51, 52,
    53, 54, 55
posture 5, 10, 18, 20, 22, 23, 25, 49, 50, 110

repetition 15, 17, 58, 124
resonance 5, 26, 35, 38, 40
rhythmic integrity 12, 13, 58

shifting 12, 22, 26, 40, 59, 69, 79, 82, 85,
    89, 95, 104, 109, 113, 114, 121, 123
shoulder rest 23, 25, 26
shoulders 18, 19, 20, 23, 25, 26, 36
spiccato 14, 22, 45, 47, 124
straight bow 24
string crossings 10, 11, 28, 45, 48, 93,
    95, 124

technique 4, 7, 8, 9, 10, 13, 20, 21, 53, 58,
    123, 124, 125
tension 4, 5, 9, 12, 15, 21, 23, 26, 29, 31,
    36, 38, 50, 51, 56, 58, 59, 79, 85, 89, 93,
    109, 124
thumb
    left 25, 26, 51, 53, 69, 79, 109
    right 29, 31, 32, 36, 37
tone 2, 3, 5, 10, 21, 26, 27, 40, 49, 53, 55,
    58, 121

vibrato 2, 11, 26, 50, 51, 52, 53, 54, 55, 58,
    59, 62, 63, 95, 106, 121, 123

weight 5, 23, 25, 27, 29, 35, 36, 40, 53, 54,
    55, 58, 79
wrist
    left 50, 51, 52, 53, 54, 56, 80, 82, 89,
    109, 114
    right 27, 29, 31, 32, 33, 34, 35, 45, 48, 49